RELIGIOUS SUPERSTITION
THROUGH THE AGES

RELIGIOUS
SUPERSTITION
through the ages

by

DON LEWIS

MOWBRAYS
LONDON & OXFORD

© A. R. Mowbray & Co Ltd 1975

Printed in Great Britain by
Western Printing Services Ltd, Bristol,

ISBN 264 66121 4

First published 1975 by
A. R. Mowbray & Co Ltd, The Alden Press,
Osney Mead, Oxford OX2 0EG

Contents

For Paul
Geoffrey Paul Savill Worsley
16 Dec. 1958 – 6 Nov. 1972

Introduction

THE DOMINANT instinct which man shares with all living creatures is self-preservation. As primitive man began to devise ways of averting the risks and dangers which everywhere threatened his survival, his actions gave expression to the views he had formulated as to the source and nature of life. He clutched at any straw which might seem to save him from danger and destruction. Man's craving for safety and prosperity led him to explore all the avenues of knowledge of life-giving and life-destruction, and to devise means of protection.

Belief in life-giving is the essential motive that underlies all supernatural beliefs, and is not only the source of superstition, but also the idea which has prompted all human progress. The early history of man was shaped and dominated by supernatural beliefs. They did not pretend to be able to explain or understand them. It was enough that there was an inherited tradition from their ancestors: they observed ceremonies and performed strange rituals which may seem to twentieth-century man unreasonable and outside the scope of the laws of nature. There can be little doubt, however, that, as these superstitions were believed in, they did in moments of crisis, danger or depression, lift men's hearts to deal with particular situations.

Roughly speaking, one would suppose that superstition declines as the view of the universe becomes more scientific, yet history in fact reveals that many superstitions were widespread amongst people who had ample opportunities for education and the acquisition of a sophisticated culture. Even when man ceased to examine the entrails of animals or observe the flight of birds or trust omens to predict future events, his behaviour was still influenced by all sorts of trivial circumstances and events that were equally lacking in reasonable justification, but were confidently held to presage good or evil.

Superstitions, from the Latin *superstes*, are those things which survive; they are the remnants of old practices, knowledge, or opinion. It is generally held that superstition is the uneducated man's inheritance of the traditional beliefs of his ancestors based on the ignorance and irrational fear surrounding the great mysteries of life. Yet so hard does superstition die that even in the twentieth century we cannot claim to be entirely free from the fetters which weighed so heavily on our forebears. While very few are prepared to acknowledge themselves superstitious, most people are ready enough to recognise superstition in others. 'What is religion to you is superstition to me', and vice versa, is a tacit assumption against which we must be on our guard. It may be also that we need to be on our guard concerning what has been termed a superstitious fear of superstition itself. While twentieth-century man is assumed to be a rational being, his actions are rarely determined by reason alone. Tradition and belief are responsible for much of his thought and action, and reason comes into play to account for behaviour which is often inspired by altogether different motives.

Bacon maintained that 'the master of superstition is the people', and we would probably add, looking back over the ages, that the master of the people is ignorance. It is a mistake, however, to assume that only the ignorant are superstitious. The love of and the desire for the mysterious and supernatural is a part of human nature, and whereas a sound education may control this, it cannot destroy it. Marx wrote to Petrus de Apono that 'superstition is so firmly imbedded in human nature, that a phrenologist might discover an organ for life'. It is reasonable to assume that the more highly educated are not likely to indulge in the more extravagant forms of superstition; nevertheless it may be true that their feelings and hopes and fears are influenced in smaller ways by smaller things, which have a very real hold on their minds and differ only in degree from the more extreme superstitious practices and beliefs.

Perhaps the most difficult question of all to answer is why some of the superstitions of the past persist in the present. One of the reasons may be that, like Christianity, superstitions are caught and not taught. They are sucked in, as it were, with our mother's or the State's milk; we learn the potency of lucky numbers at father's knee as he fills in the pools coupon; we breathe the atmosphere of hippy amulets sported by older brothers and sisters; mother touches wood for luck; grandmother mutters 'Bless you' at every sneeze—and all at a time of growing up when our young minds are receptive and impressionable.

It appears also that there is such a thing as a superstitious mind, quite independent of education and training. The classic example is Dr Johnson, who believed that unless he touched every post as he walked down a street something unfortunate would happen. Irrational it may be, but once such an idea is imbedded in the mind it is seldom, if ever, completely eradicated.

An important reason for superstitions still persisting is that they are associated with those realms which modern science tends to dismiss or explain away. They are an exaggeration of what many would term a reasonable belief in some supernatural agents or agencies. There is at the heart of all religions a supernatural element, but, quite apart from this, many superstitions that are alien to the higher religions persist amongst people living in an enlightened scientific environment. It may be that, as chemistry grew out of alchemy, and astronomy out of astrology, the superstitions associated with the supernatural and occultism will ultimately lead to discoveries in mental science which will be of infinitely greater value for the well-being of mankind.

CHAPTER ONE

Fear and Fertility

WHAT COULD the Easter egg, Midsummer's Day, the blazing
Yuletide log, dancing round the Maypole and heaven being up
there in the sky have in common? Nowadays we smile at these
quaint appendices in our society and think no more about them.
In its early days of establishment, however, the Christian
Church found it necessary to harness these superstitions firmly
with the sanctifying bridle of the cross, since they implied uncompromising philandering with the primitive worship of the
fertility cult and similar naïve beliefs in the gods of nature.
And the reason for these notions was the fundamental assertion
that the basic elements of the universe, like the sky, the earth,
fire, water, blood, growing trees and the frightening inscrut-
ability of the elements, all possessed divine power: power to
destroy life and also to ensure its continuation.

THE SACRED TREE

Quite apart from the prominence Adam and Eve gave trees
when they ate the fruit of the tree of Knowledge of Good and
Evil in the Semitic Creation Story, trees and tree-worship are
one of the basic elements in the structure of ancient faiths. In
the very earliest age man started out as his own god, in the
sense that he believed in no control of nature other than his
own. He looked to no higher power than himself for help in
making rain or enabling his trees to be fruitful. This is far removed from belief in a higher being whose aid must be sought
or bought. Even to this day in primitive tribes, imitative magic
such as beating drums to simulate thunder, or pouring out water
in imitation of rain, is not uncommon in order to bring a drought
to an end. Those people who practise this imitative magic are
not attempting to evoke a higher power; they believe that the
resemblance will suffice to produce the reality. Frazer in *The*

Golden Bough records that in Bohemia the first apple produced by a tree is sometimes picked and eaten by a woman who has given birth to many children; this is done in order that the young tree shall become, in the gardener's phrase, 'a good cropper'.

Trees have played a conspicuous part in all religious systems —Persian, Hindu, Arabian, Chinese, Assyrian, and Babylonian. In Britain the oak has ever been regarded with special significance. There was a time when it was generally believed that an oak groaned and shrieked as it was being felled, and that these sounds were made by the spirit which inhabited the tree. This belief is clearly seen in Teutonic mythology: 'Temple means also wood,' says Grimm in his *Teutonic Mythology*. 'What we figure to ourselves as a built and walled house resolves itself, the further back we go, into a holy place untouched by human hand embowered and shut in by self-grown trees. There dwells the deity, veiling his form in the rustling foliage of the boughs.'

The Old Testament gives evidence of tree-worship: the *Ashera* of the Canaanites was not a grove, but a tree or post, and the tree or post occurs frequently in connection with divine appearances. So Yahweh appeared to Abraham beneath the oak tree in Mamre, and to Moses in the burning bush. Joshua at Shechem 'took a great stone, and set it up there under an oak, that was by the sanctuary of the Lord.' Deborah the Prophetess 'dwelt under the palm tree of Deborah in Mount Ephraim, and the children of Israel came to her for judgement.' Also from the Old Testament narrative, we have evidence that trees were regarded as an oracle or medium of communication between gods and men. Thus the voice of God came to Moses from the burning bush. David, when he enquired of the Lord how and when he should attack the Philistines, was commanded 'not to go up; but to go around to their rear and come upon them opposite the balsam trees.' And then, at the sound of 'marching in the tops of the balsam trees,' was he to move, for that was the sign that Yahweh was before Israel's army ready to smite the host of the Philistines.

In Europe the trees most surrounded by superstition are the rowan or mountain ash, the thorn, and the elder. A twig of the last, silently laid on the ground, was commonly used in Denmark as a cure for toothache. At the same time, however, no cradle was ever made from the elder since conviction held this tree to be under the protection of Elder-mother, without whose consent not even a leaf might be touched. In pre-Christian times, the Prussian earth-god was thought to live under the elder tree, and the legend that this wood was used for the cross on which Christ was crucified was an attempt to give Christian colour to a heathen practice.

MAYPOLE MERRIMENT

May Day ceremonies in origin were religious observances, believed to secure the blessings which the spirits could bestow. The spirit which inhabited the tree also inhabited the maypole taken from the tree; hence the dance around the maypole was a religious ceremony. The May Queen and Jack-in-the-Green were, in origin, human forms of the tree's spirit. The belief was that the maypole conserved fertility, both in cattle and human beings—a persuasion not yet extinct in many parts of Europe. These superstitions connected with merrymaking in May can be traced back to Roman sources to a ceremony credited to Claudius. This festivity was held in honour of Maia, the mother of Mercury, at Ostia, a town about sixteen miles from Rome, and later it was incorporated with Floralia, the feast of Flora, the goddess of flowers, which was held on 27 April and lasted for several days. *Floralia* was for the special enjoyment of women, and they ran races day and night in the amphitheatre, the winners being garlanded with flowers. Besides these floral decorations they were also besieged with whole trees which, after felling, the gallants of Rome took and set up at the doors of their mistresses. In the process of time, however, trees became too cumbersome, and instead tall poles with garlands were substituted.

In *Anatomy of Abuses*, a Puritan diatribe of 1583, Philip Stubbs describes the maypole as being 'covered all over with flowers and herbs, bound round about with strings from the top to the bottom, and sometimes painted with variable colours, with two or three hundred men, women and children following it with great devotion. And thus being reared up with handkerchiefs and flags streaming on the top, they strewed the ground about, plaited green boughs around it, set up summer-halls, bowers, and arbours hard by it; and then fell to banquet and feast, leaping and dancing about it as the heathen people did at the dedication of their idols, whereof this was a perfect pattern, or indeed the thing itself.'

During Easter Week in 1282 an isolated incident occurred in Scotland which revealed that, even after hundreds of years of repression, fertility cults were still capable of commanding the support of people. This support was shown in the miming of springtime fertility rites and was defended as the exercise of religious and social privilege. The Chronicle of Lanercost recorded that the Priest of Inverkeithing, named John, 'revived the profane rites of Priapus, collecting young girls from the villages and compelling them to dance in circles to the honour of Father Bacchus. When he had these females in a troop, out of sheer wantonness he led the dance, carrying before them on a pole a representation of the human organs of reproduction; and singing and dancing himself, like a mime, he reviewed them all and stirred them to lust by filthy language.' (Priapus was once regarded as one of the lesser fertility gods who was to be served with dancing to ensure fecundity of humans as well as of crops and animals.)

Thus evolved the customs surrounding the maypole. In our day, dancing round the maypole is smiled upon as a quaint and pretty custom, a time for children to dress up and dance round it. There is no more significance to the performance than there is to the crowning of the Rosebud Queen. All is bland innocence. Yet in 1644 Parliament was forced to issue an order for the destruction of the maypole 'because the prophanation of the Lord's Day hath been heretofore greatly occasioned by Maypoles (a heathenish vanity, generally abused to superstition and wickedness) the Lords and Commons do further order and ordain that all and singular May-poles, that are or shall be erected, shall be taken down and removed by the constables, borsholders, tything-men, petty constables, and churchwardens of the parishes, where the same shall be; and that no May-pole shall be hereafter set up, erected, or suffered to be within this kingdom of England, or dominion of Wales. The said officers in case of default, to be fined five shillings weekly till the said May-pole be taken down.'

After the Restoration and the return of less sober times, however, the maypole was permitted to return in all its glory, and once more the frolic was on.

'Come, lasses and lads, take leave of your dads,
    And away to the May-pole hie;
For every he has got him a she,
    And the minstrel's standing by;
For Willie has gotten his Jill,
    And Johnny has got his Joan,
To jig it, jig it, jig it,
    Jig it up and down.'

HEAVENLY DWELLING

In the fancies of early mankind, earth, forests, running water, and hills were the dwelling-places of the deities. 'The Aka feared the high mountains which towered aloft over his dwelling; he feared the roaring torrents of the deep glen, which interposed between him and his friends beyond; and he feared the dark and dense jungle in which his cattle lost their way. These dark and threatening powers of nature he invested with the supernatural attributes; they were his gods, and he named them Fúxo, the god of jungle and water; Firan and Siman, the gods of war; and Satu, the god of house and field. Offerings are made to the gods at different cultivating seasons, and also in token of gratitude when a child was born.' (Dalton, *Ethnology of Bengal.*)

Generally, however, it was the sky that took precedence amongst primitive societies as the source of life-giving substances. Regarded as a vast repository, it was also looked upon as an actual place to which the dead were taken. Thus grew the problems of early theologians, having to try to explain the physical means whereby such transference was effected. Another belief associated with the sky was that which asserted that it was possible to predict from the heavenly bodies not only the ordinary events of life such as the succession of the seasons, the movements of tides and the periods of harvest, but also the destinies of men and women.

This represented the general characteristics of nature—worship existing in more or less degree all over the world. Its extreme form took the view that God is all and all is God, and while the word 'pantheist' was probably coined by the Deist John Tolland in 1705, the antiquity of this mode of belief is great and was prevalent in the oldest known civilisations of the world. Neither America, France, nor England has produced a

great pantheistic philosopher; but an immense amount of
pantheistic sentiment has floated about in the theology and
poetry in the European culture down the ages. It was Words-
worth who penned:

'And I have felt
A presence that disturbs me with the joy
Of elevated thoughts; a sense sublime
Of something far more deeply interfused,
Whose dwelling is the light of setting suns,
And the round ocean and the living air,
And the blue sky, and in the mind of man;
A motion and a spirit, that impels
All thinking things, all objects of all thought,
And rolls through all things.'
(*Lines composed a few Miles above Tintern Abbey*)

Regard for the heavenly bodies was also acknowledged by
the Druids in their festivals which were regulated by the moon
and the sun. Thus, Mayday Eve, Midsummer Eve, All Hallow-
e'-en and Yule were the major festivals of Druidical worship,
on which occasions fires and sacrifices were offered to the sun-
god Beal. In these ritual observances, the Druids were at pains
to cater for the multitude, those whose grosser senses, they
argued, required such acknowledgement. In the same way, their
veneration for groves and the oak, and for sacred fountains, was
an expression of natural worship. Their belief in the sanctity of
the mistletoe, and the watch-fires of Spring, Summer and
Autumn, were tributes to the bounty of the All-giver who, they
believed, was the sole promoter of the growth, ripening and
harvesting of the fruits of the earth.

This subtle emphasis on one god was the only concession they
made to the masses of this secret belief of theirs. In the main,
they deemed it sufficient, and indeed better, that the simple
folk should be polytheists, maintaining that their own doctrine
of belief in one god should be reserved for the initiated alone.
Such is the maintenance of some scholars.

The religious system of the Druids, as seen by Diogenes
Laertius, however, was based, quite simply, on the three main
precepts: to worship the gods, to do no evil, and to act with
courage. But whatever their creed, there is little doubt about

the form their outward worship took. It was, basically, founded upon regard for the heavenly bodies and regulated by the sun and moon. Perhaps it is more than coincidence therefore that the Church thought fit to make Midsummer's day (the day on which the Druids' Great Festival took place and on which feasting and fires and dancing in the round was the common order), the festival of John the Baptist. It was intended that the fires should symbolise John, for John was a shining light, and it was he who preceded the True Light, Jesus.

FIRE FESTIVAL

From the same foundations grew the custom in Ireland that bonfires should blaze on every hill and in every farmyard on St John's Eve, 23 June. A field into which a burning brand had not been thrown was considered barren, and it was essential that every horse and cow be touched by fire on that night. At the beginning of the nineteenth century, the Rev. Dr McQueen of Kilmuir, in the Isle of Skye, visited Ireland and recorded that, 'The Irish have ever been worshippers of fire and of Baal, and are so to this day. The chief festival in honour of the sun and fire is upon the 21st June, when the sun arrives at the summer solstice, or rather begins its retrograde motion.' He described the baal fires which he saw, in these words: 'I was so fortunate in the summer of 1782 as to have my curiosity gratified. At the house where I was entertained it was told me that we should see at midnight the most singular sight in Ireland, which was the lighting of fires in honour of the sun. Accordingly, exactly at midnight, the fires began to appear; and going up to the leads of the house, which had a widely extended view, I saw, on a radius of 30 miles, all round, the fire burning on every eminence which the country afforded. I had a further satisfaction of learning, from undoubted authority, that the people danced round the fires, and at the close, went through these fires, and made their sons and daughters, together with their cattle, pass through the fire, and the whole was concluded with religious solemnity.'

Fire in private dwellings was supplied from a sacred fire consecrated by the Druids, and these, once extinguished, could not be rekindled until the tithes due from the household were paid. The translation of this practice by the early Christians to

Old Christmas Day, the Epiphany, was a fair substitute. The fire was seen to symbolise the star which led the Magi, while the money with which it could be purchased represented the offerings of the Wise Men.

'It was an auncient ordinaunce, that noo man sholde come to God, ne to the Kyng, with a voyde honde, but that he brought some gyfte.' (*The Golden Legend*.)

That the purchase of fire should last for twelve days is also in accord with ancient superstition, since the observance of twelve days was associated with the Saturnalia, and at Rome on New Year's Day, no householder would allow a neighbour to take fire out of his house, or any thing of iron, or to lend anything.

This superstition surrounding fire was not only found in Europe. As far away as North America, similar beliefs were maintained. Thus, the Sioux during their sacred feasts used to extinguish all fire from their lodges and kindle fresh fire before cooking, so that there would be nothing unclean at the feast.

Bonfire celebrations in the Autumn have been held since pagan times, and probably derived from the ancient festival of Samhain, which was celebrated on 31 October. The ancient pagan year was divided into two main periods—Winter, which commenced on 1 November, and Summer; and both these periods were preceded by the kindling of fire and the lighting of ceremonial fires. These bonfires lasted long after paganism had been superseded and they were seen in many countries blazing on May Day Eve, Midsummer Eve, and Hallowe'en. Many of the Samhain ceremonies were transferred to other winter celebrations; Christmas, Twelfth Night and New Year's Day all show traces of sun- and fire-worship—the lighted Christmas tree, the blazing Christmas pudding, the yule log and the lighted candles.

MUNDANE EGGS

Sun- and fire-worship, therefore, can be seen to have played a major part in primitive religion through the ages. The Semitic custom of passing children through fire existed wherever the human mind grasped the concept of sacrifice and purification. Also connected with the new-birth idea was the presence of eggs at these rites and mysteries. Superstition surrounding the egg is at least as ancient as these early heathen festivals. Many ancient nations believed that the world itself was in fact egg-shaped, and indeed, that it was hatched from an egg made by the Creator. According to Hindu superstition the world was thought to have existed in embryo in the mind of Brahm, until the actual moment of creation; Brahm spoke, and light appeared, matter filled up space, water condensed and vegetation began to grow. Again Brahm spoke and there appeared a golden egg, in which were the three emblems of birth, fertility, and death, or wisdom, power, and destruction, in the forms of the gods Brahma, Vishnu, and Siva. When this golden egg hatched, its shell was thought to have shattered into fourteen pieces; seven ascending to form the superior worlds; seven descending to form as many inferior ones.

An ancient Japanese superstition maintains that the world was created from a cock's egg. A giant from this world, who had conquered heaven, made a woman, and she, by mating with a crocodile, became the mother of the human race. So deeply was this believed that the family of the Congues wore tails to their breeches in honour of their supposed origin.

The Hawaiians believed that the island of Hawaii was created by the hatching of an egg which had been laid on the waters by a huge bird. In fact all the nations of antiquity—the Egyptians, Persians, Romans, Greeks, Gauls and others—regarded the egg as an emblem of the universe—a work of the supreme Divinity. The ancient Britons abstained from eating eggs, because to do so would be to destroy the vital principle in embryo. 'Everything springs from the egg, it is the world's cradle,' declared the oracle of the Druids; and indeed, as one of the badges of his office, every Druid had an egg encased in gold hung about his neck. Describing it, Pliny wrote, 'it is about the bigness of a moderate apple; its shell is a cartilaginous incrustation, full of little cavities, such as are on the legs of the polypus.'

CHRISTIANISED SUPERSTITION

The persistence of heathen superstitions surrounding fertility and fear of the unknown owes much to the advent of world religions. Even the coming of Christianity, whose teachings opposed the religions of the period, in fact Christianised many of the old superstitions, rather than ban them. 'The Bretons', claimed St Gregory, as he persuaded his missionaries to purify and not destroy, 'have fixed days for feasts and sacrifices; leave them their feasts and do not restrain their sacrifices; leave them the joy of their festivals, only from the state of paganism draw them gently and progressively into the estate of Christ.'

Easter was celebrated at the time of the solar New Year—the day of renewal for all living things—the incubation of nature. The egg was seen by early Christians as a symbol of the resurrection, and the practice of giving coloured pasch eggs on Easter morning seems to have been part of an ancient custom, which was taken over by the Church. This practice altered little in various countries over the centuries. There was a time in Russia when, on Easter Day, the peasants carried eggs coloured red to denote the blood of Christ (while the gentry had theirs gilded), so that 'when two friends meete during the Easter Holydayes, they come and take one another by the hand; the one of them saith, "The Lord, or Christ is risen!" The other answereth, "It is so of a trueth," and then they kiss and exchange their egges.' (Hakluyt's *Voyages*, 1589.)

The triumph of Christianity over paganism resulted not only in the survival of ancient superstitions by the sanctification of pagan rites and festivals but also in becoming the source of a whole group of new ones. The historical events of the birth, life and death of Christ and his early followers provided a basis for these new superstitions, and although discountenanced by the Church, they rapidly became embedded in the minds of the people. Thus, when the first Christian missionaries lived and worked amongst the Celtic races they impressed their uneducated neighbours by the holy lives they led and the brave way in which they endured hardship and persecution. These attributes were exalted in verse and song and those men, looked upon as moral giants, grew, by succeeding generations, to be regarded as physical giants also. Add to this the way in which the early priesthood persuaded people of their miraculous powers, and it is not difficult to see how ordinary men became extraordinary heroes and saints. Curious superstitions gripped simple folk, and we hear how saints were able to carry enormous boulders in their pockets, hurl them into the air and, because of these feats, had churches dedicated to their memory.

CHAPTER TWO

Love and Marriage

LOVE AND MARRIAGE being a natural upshot of one of the facts of life, it follows that superstition will have a generous hand where they are concerned. From choosing the right partner, through the hazardous period of courtship and over the threshold of the new life together, charms, traditions and taboo play a colourful part. Again traces of the great primaries can be found, such as the love charms evolved from the wooden pillars, fire, and the sprinkling of blood. Evil spirits have to be guarded against, benign spirits propitiated, and all through, and amongst the newer derivations like the rice and red carpet, the lovers' knots, the rings and crowns, and the shoe of authority, there is woven the hallowing thread of the Christian Church to give meaning to the gay charade.

LOVE-PROVOKING

In the history of mankind long before the use of gold, shells took precedence as the standard currency, and possessed as well a magical significance. The cowrie shell became regarded as a symbol of the life-giving powers of women and in process of time it was used as an amulet credited with power to protect the living from death, and to confer upon the dead a prolongation of existence. It is even now the practice of girls in Africa and in the islands of the Pacific to wear girdles of cowrie shells. In early times this custom was more widespread and was a common practice in India and Central America; indeed some ancient statues show that cowries were worn by both men and women. Moving from their completely naked state to that of wearing shells or leaves suspended from girdles, men discovered that such decoration added to a girl's allure. Thus the magic girdle evolved into a love-provoking charm. When Ishtar, the goddess of love and war and mother of all life in the Babylonian epics, removed her girdle, all reproduction was halted. Aphrodite's girdle was believed to be capable of compelling love. The Garden of Eden narrative in the Old Testament suggests that Eve's girdle of fig leaves was the prototype of all clothing. Cowries to this day are used as girdles by Polynesian girls partly as a garment of attraction and partly because of the magic attributed to them: they are to be found in use as ornaments for women's dresses in Borneo and Africa and also as an integral part of the witch doctor's bundle of tricks. With time, and where cowrie shells could not be found, other means took over in the superstitious practices surrounding love. Gradually there evolved a confused mixture of sacrifice, astrology, sympathetic magic and Christianity, to determine the name of a lover, the course of true love, and the most propitious time to marry.

Even the aid of St Peter was sought by young women wishing to know the fate of their love-life! The maidens of Rome in olden days used a charm which found its way to England and was being advocated as late as the second half of the nineteenth century.

'Get nine small keys of your own, make a three-plaited band of your own hair, and tie them together, fastening the ends with nine knots. Then with a garter, fasten them to your left wrist, and on going to bed bind the other garter round your head and say,

> St Peter, take it not amiss,
> To try your favour I've done this;
> You are the ruler of the keys,
> Favour me then if you please;
> Let me then your influence prove,
> And see my dear and wedded love.'

Brand records a delightful piece of divination to be carried out on All Souls' Eve, if a woman wished to know her success in getting the husband of her choice. It runs like an old cookery recipe and needs only the addition, 'First catch your swain and truss him'.

'Get two lemon-peels, wear them all day, and one in each pocket and at night rub the four posts of the bed-stead with them.' If success were forthcoming, the swain would appear in the suppliant's sleep and present her with a couple of lemons;

if not, there was no hope. A superstitious way of choosing a wife was to find out the birthday of the young woman of your choice, and then consult the last chapter of the Book of Proverbs. Each verse, from the first to the thirty-first, was supposed to indicate directly, or indirectly, the character of the woman selected: finally the verse corresponding with her age was regarded as indication of the woman's true character.

NAMING THE DAY

In ancient times the sacredness of the house was always safeguarded. The secrecy attached to courtship in olden days bears witness to this fact in some measure. In parts of the country, when a youth visited his sweetheart in her home, it was nearly always after the family had gone to bed, the fire had been darkened and the candle extinguished. He cautiously entered the house and remained with his sweetheart for a few hours. The parents of the girl knew very well what was going on, but it was not until the couple had named the day for their marriage, and when it was known that the girl's parents had no objection to the match, that the man dared show himself openly in the house. There was a time among the peasants of Brittany when there was no betrothal ceremony as such, but after a match had been arranged by a go-between, the lover and the girl would eat a meal from a common plate. This primitive rite of union survived in various forms in different parts of Europe and was surrounded by superstition, since it was believed that if the common meal was interrupted in any way the couple's children would be born with cross-eyes or a humpback. In some countries the time of betrothal was a period when evil spirits were exceptionally active and engaged couples particularly vulnerable. In Bavaria it was considered a sign of ill fortune if a bride picked up anything lying in her path, and she was never allowed to come into contact with the dead or dying. Five crosses were sewn on to the cover of the marriage-bed to ward off spells cast by witches, and the first thing the bride carried into her new home was a crucifix. Even during this century there have been found strange survivals of the courting ritual of bygone days. It was thought in Sweden that if a lad and a maid ate of the same loaf of bread they were sure to fall in love with one another. In Western Gothland the woman had to give her husband-to-be a shirt made with her own hands, which he must wear on his wedding-day but not again until the day he died when he was buried in it. The man must never give his lover a sharp instrument since it would sever his love; or a handkerchief since this would wipe away her friendship for him; or a pair of shoes, for this would symbolise that she would walk away from him.

The superstition that it is unlucky to get married at certain times of the year is one of those which has descended to Christianity from Pagan observances. The Romans believed the month of May to be unpropitious for marriage. Plutarch gives three reasons for this: first, because May is between April which is the month of Venus, and June which is consecrated to Juno, both deities being considered propitious to marriage and therefore not be slighted. Secondly, because of the major expiatory celebration of the *Lemuria* when females abstained from the bath and from using cosmetics, essentials in pre-marriage rituals. Thirdly, because May was the old men's month, *Majus a Majoribus*, whereas June was the month of the young, *Junius a Junioribus*. The close seasons of the year for marriage were anciently from Advent to St Hilary's Day (13 January), Septuagesima to Low Sunday and Rogation Sunday to Trinity Sunday.

> Advent marriage doth deny,
> But Hilary gives the liberty.
> Septuagesima says thee nay,
> Eight days from Easter says you may.
> Rogation bids thee to contain,
> But Trinity sets thee free again.

While these restrictions lapsed during the Commonwealth period they were generally observed throughout the sixteenth and seventeenth centuries.

In olden days in the South and West of Ireland marriages among the peasantry usually took place during Shrovetide. Indeed, it was considered unlucky to be married at any other time of the year. Thus, whenever possible, a priest visited the island of Tory for the purpose of solemnising any wedding which had been arranged. Some years, however, it happened that the weather was so stormy at that season that a boat could not approach the island for weeks on end, and when this occurred, the engaged couple would stand on the east shore of the island, while a priest standing on the shore of the mainland opposite them read the marriage ceremony across the water. As soon as the weather permitted, the priest went to the island and did whatever was necessary to render the marriages valid in the eyes of the law and of the church.

WEDDING RITUAL

In the northern countries of England in ancient times a knot was considered a symbol of love. Knots or bows of ribbon, symbolising the indissoluble tie of love and duty, came to be used as wedding favours and were known as True Lovers' Knots. These favours in the form of ribbons were worn on the hat in England, whereas in France the bridal favour was worn on the arm. In ancient Babylon at marriage a thread was drawn from the wedding garments of both bride and groom and the two threads were knotted together to symbolise the union. Even to this day marriage is referred to as 'tying the knot', and the custom in many churches for the priest to bind the end of his stole around the hands of the bride and bridegroom when he utters the words, 'Those whom God hath joined together let no man put asunder' seems to be connected with the superstition which surrounds 'tying the knot'. It would appear that this ritual is an innovation by the priests, since there is no direction for this ritual in the Book of Common Prayer or in the standard Roman or Sarum Missals. The bridal wreath worn in marriage comes from ancient times: Roman brides wore chaplets of flowers, and at Saxon weddings both bride and groom wore wreaths. Saracen women used orange blossom and Norse brides wore golden marriage crowns.

The placing of the wedding ring on the fourth finger of the left hand is based on the superstition that on that finger is a certain vein which proceeds to the heart. This ritual implied that the contracting parties with their hands made also an interchange of hearts. Some authorities maintain that the ring is an earnest; others maintain it to be a pledge of fidelity. Ancient canon law recognised the false impression that a vein from the fourth finger of the left hand ran immediately to the heart. This medical opinion, however, is primitive and is certainly that of very ancient Egypt and Greece. An amatory charm consisted in drawing a circle with the blood from the fourth finger on a wafer which was afterwards consecrated. Among gypsy peoples, a feature of marriage is the mingling of the blood of both bride and bridegroom, who either hold hands or have their wrists bound together. It is sometimes also the custom that they eat a cake into which drops of blood from each of them have been mixed.

Wedding rings were used both by the Greeks and Romans, though they were bestowed at the time of betrothal and not at the marriage ceremony itself. In Anglo-Saxon times, the bridegroom made a pledge at the betrothal and placed a ring on the maiden's right hand, where it remained until the marriage, when it was transferred to the left. The exchange of the ring on to the left hand was probably encouraged because the virgins espoused to the Church wore the rings of their celestial nuptials on the right hand. In the Middle Ages, rings were thought to have magical properties and were often worn as talismans against evil. Each stone was thought to have special significance. Diamonds, for instance, were supposed to stand for innocence, and rubies for love and understanding, which is quite possibly why they have always been such a popular choice for engagement rings.

The kiss once common in the ceremonial attending marriage has now been relegated to a hasty peck in the vestry or a pose for the photographer. The nuptial kiss, however, was once a solemn ceremony performed before the altar. A pall, or care-cloth, was held over the couple, and after they had received the nuptial blessing the care-cloth was removed and the bridegroom received the kiss of peace from the priest, whereupon he kissed his bride. The bridal veil is a pale reflection of the care-cloth, and the nuptial kiss has barely survived except in remote rural areas where it is still considered a good luck omen to kiss the parson immediately after the marriage ceremony.

In many parts of the world the bride and groom in the marriage ceremony are looked upon as royalties—that is of divine or sacred character. In Polynesia the bride and groom were regarded as being sacred, which made it taboo for them to walk on the ground, and so they were carried to the marriage ceremony. (Does this have a connection with the bridal car of today?) The final act of ritual in the marriage ceremonies in Tahiti was to throw a cloth over the bride and groom, a feature of marriage ceremonial which appears to have been widespread. This cloth, together with the garments they wore at the marriage ceremony, were for ever after considered to be sacred. In some Scandinavian communities a canopy or covering is placed not only over the table where the bride and groom sit for the meal after the wedding ceremony but also over the nuptial bed. This was thought to protect the couple from evil spirits, which was also probably the origin of the bride and groom holding lighted candles with crowns held over their heads in the marriage ceremonies of the Greek Orthodox Church. The Russian peoples also, at one time, set great store by the use of crowns during the marriage ceremony, and it has been suggested that it is a form of disguise to protect the couple from evil spirits. The Nordic races, however, regarded the silver crown or head-dress as a symbol of chastity. It was considered important that the shoes of the bride should have neither buckle, button nor strap if she would have easy delivery of her first-born.

TRANSFERENCE OF AUTHORITY

'On leaving his house, it was customary for the bridegroom to have thrown after him an old shoe and, in like manner, an old shoe after the bride when she left her home to proceed to church. This was done to ensure good luck to each respectively; and if by stratagem either of the bride's shoes could be taken off by any spectator on her way from the church, it had to be ransomed by the bridegroom' (Train. *History of the Isle of Man*).

In South China it was the practice of the bride to give her husband a pair of shoes. In the seventeenth century it was the practice in England, 'when at any time a couple were married, that the sole of the bridegroom's shoe should be laid on the bride's head' (Thrupp. *Anglo-Saxon Home*, 1640).

Brand, in his *Popular Antiquities*, records that it is considered lucky by the vulgar to throw an old shoe after a person when they wish him to succeed in some new venture he is setting out on. This ceremony of throwing an old 'left' shoe after a person was not restricted to marriage but was a general luck-wishing superstition practised in olden days when anyone left home.

Among primitive peoples, transference of property and possessions and assertions and relinquishment of rights were, in the absence of legal documents, marked by some external rite or ceremony. When land was bought or sold in Scandinavia a turf was given by the seller to the purchaser, while in oriental nations, a shoe was used for this purpose. Among the Jews, the widow of a childless man could not marry again until she had been refused marriage by her husband's brother. If the woman was refused publicly in open court (Deut. 25.7-9) 'she loosed his shoe from off his foot, and spat before his face'. The giving up of a shoe showed that the brother refused to take up the option on 'the first refusal', and her spitting before his face was a symbolic act of her assertion of independence. The Old Testament story of the widow Ruth reveals how her nearest kinsman took off his shoe and gave it to Boaz as a public renunciation of all dominion over her, and of his right of pre-marriage. The giving of a bride's shoe to the groom by the girl's father showed that he was renouncing dominion and authority over her, and the receipt of the shoe by the bride-groom was an indication that he accepted the transferred authority. Indeed, it was not unusual for the groom to tap his bride on the head with it, to exercise that authority as soon as possible! In these days the use of the shoe at marriage has been relegated to being tied to the back of the honeymoon car and occasionally as miniature luck charms on or around the wedding cake.

> But, 'When Britons bold,
>   Wedded of old,
> Sandals were backward thrown,
>   The pair to tell,
>   That, ill or well,
> The act was all their own.' (Old Rhyme)

The idea of luck is the principal thought associated with the shoe superstition in recent centuries, especially luck in making journeys.

Marriage was a time when spirits were thought to be unusually active, and for this reason in New Britain, when arrangements had been made for a marriage, the bridegroom hid himself in the bush until the marriage feast was due to take place. Protective measures had to be taken when bringing two people together in what was considered, at a magical level, a dangerous relationship. Thus, when the Papuans of Long Island performed a wedding ceremony, it was in a room set apart for the purpose, with the bride and groom standing back to back surrounded by their friends, men on one side, women on the other. An old man then joined their right hands together and spat a mouthful of water over the couple chanting, 'May no enemy kill you, may no evil spirit affect you with sickness.' The husband and wife and their guests then partook of sago, and for four nights the pair had to sit up watched by their friends, who did not allow them to fall asleep. This was considered to be a precaution against attack from evil spirits and was a discipline carried out to ensure a long and prosperous life. Only on the fifth night were the bride and groom allowed to be alone.

Feasting was closely associated with most religious ceremonies, and more often than not specific food became associated with a particular feast. Thus, small cakes made of flour, salt, spices, water, and honey were consumed at the bridal feast. The Celtic goddess Brid or Bridget is regarded by some authorities as the prototype of St Bride, to whom so many churches in Wales are dedicated. Brid is more than likely the deity from whom the English derived their word 'bride' for a woman in the marriage ceremony. Brid was regarded as the protective goddess of marriage, and among the ancient Irish the sacrifice on the occasion of a marriage was termed *Caca-Brideoige*, or the *Cake of Brid*. It is likely that our present day wedding-cake with its attendant superstitions, on the day of a marriage, originated from this idolatrous sacrificial rite. The wedding-cake, made with the richest possible ingredients and surmounted with layers of sweet icing and bitter almond paste, is symbolic of the bitter-sweet, pleasure-pain relationship of every marriage.

The first period after the marriage is termed the honeymoon. This derives from the practice once common to all the northern European nations, when at the marriage of the chiefs people indulged in thirty days of drinking a liquor made from honey.

OVER THE THRESHOLD

Among the ancient Romans fire and water were placed upon

the bridegroom's threshold, and this ancient superstition persisted in Britain, where the bride was not allowed to step on
the threshold when entering the bridegroom's house, but was
usually lifted over by her nearest relations. In addition she was
to 'knit her fillets' to the door-posts and anoint the sides, 'to
avoid the mischievious fascinations of witches'. Crossing the
threshold has ever been an important ceremony connected with
marriage, the bride having to be lifted over. In some primitive
societies, as was the case in Fiji, this reverence for the threshold
was limited to the temple or a chief's house, and the feet were
never to come into contact with it, persons of high rank striding
over it, while others crossed on hands and knees. In parts of
Britain a kettleful of boiling water was poured over the door-
step of the bride's home as she left it, the superstition being
that this was done to ensure that the remaining unmarried
children would receive proposals of marriage.

In Sicily wheat was thrown over the bride's head as she
entered her future home, and she was on no account allowed to
touch the threshold. In China, where rice was used in place of
wheat, the threshold was covered with a red cloth to prevent
its coming into contact with the bride's feet, of which tradition
the red carpet at weddings in Britain is reminiscent. Superstitions surrounding the threshold seem to be world-wide where
marriage is concerned: even among the redskin tribes of America
the bride was lifted over the threshold of her husband's dwelling.
Even to this day it is considered essential in certain parts of
the country that the bridegroom should carry the bride over
the threshold of their new home. Some people believe this to be
a survival of marriage by capture, but it is more likely that the
threshold of a house was sacred to the Goddess of Chastity,
Vesta, and therefore not to be walked on by the bride.

CHAPTER THREE

Hearth and Home

THE LIGHT-HEARTED eye we turn upon the cupboard holding its skeleton, or the almost blind eye we turn to the corner-stones and hearths are telling indictments of our attitude to ancient tradition. Nevertheless, we might be forgiven this indifference, for it is not widely publicised any longer that their origins are so meaningful. Not many people are aware that tradition demanded sacrifice at the start of any building enterprise, and that corner-stones were laid in blood-mixed mortar, reminiscent of the primitive custom of building a human sacrifice into a wall. The sentimental hearth as the home's centre became such because of the sacred fire burning there, while the derided skeleton was once regarded as essential for protection of the home, symbolic of the solicitous haunting spirit. Superstitious tradition still bade householders be wary, nevertheless, for taboo was rife not only in domestic life but in the upbringing of children also. Childhood was found to be snared with bees, nail-pairings, gooseberries and complicated birthday wishes, culminating in the rite of circumcision at the threshold of adulthood. The moon, so closely bound up with women, cast its spell upon their unborn children, and the newly delivered infant was hedged about with hazards from the unseen world —evil spirits which could only be effectively dispelled through Christian Baptism.

FIRM FOUNDATIONS

The old English proverb 'Every Englishman's house is his castle' probably derives from the superstition held by primitive society that the house is sacred. House-worship with its belief in the spirit rule by deceased ancestors, is deeply embedded in primitive society. The secrecy surrounding the primitive house-hold, with its emphasis on the worship of the hearth, and the sacredness of the threshold, seems to be the basis for so many superstitions where the protection of the house from the spirit world is concerned.

Gibbon maintains that among the pagan festivals which persisted after the establishment of the Christian religion throughout the Roman Empire was that of decorating doorways with lamps and laurel branches to indicate their protection by the household gods. In the same way, to stumble at the threshold was considered a most ominous sign. Shakespeare refers to this superstition when he puts these words into the mouth of Gloucester:

> 'For many men that stumble at the threshold
> Are well foretold that danger lurks within.'
>
> (III *Henry VI*, iv.7)

H. M. Stanley, describing the dwelling of the peasant of Uganda, mentions that in the outer court was 'a small square hut, sacred to the genius of the family, the household Muzimu. This genius, by the dues paid to him, seems to be no very exacting or avaricious spirit, for the simplest things, such as snail-shells, moulded balls of clay, certain compounds of herbs, small bits of juniper wood, and a hartebeest horn pointed with iron and stuck into the earth, suffice to propitiate him' (*Through the Dark Continent.* 1890).

In early times the spiritual centre of the house was the fire and hearth. The holy fire was never allowed to go out since fire was sacred. The power regarded as necessary to make fire was jealously guarded by the priests in the days when matches and flints were unknown, and on certain holy days a new fire was made and all household fires were put out. The house fires were then rekindled by laboriously carrying fire from house to house.

There was a time in England when all the household fires were allowed to go out on Easter Sunday, when the chimneys and fireplaces were cleaned, and the fire was once more kindled. The ancient belief that the fire must on no account go out was observed fanatically by some of the tribes of the North American Indians, where fire was kept burning day and night. Formerly in the Isle of Man 'Not a family in the whole island, but kept a fire constantly burning. It was also the rigid belief that if it should ever happen that no fires were to be found throughout the Island, the most terrible revolutions and mischiefs would immediately ensue' (Train. *History of Isle of Man*).

It is said that in every one's house there is a skeleton. More colloquially we would say that every man has a skeleton in his cupboard! In fact, however, it was at one time true that every house did in fact, literally, possess a skeleton and was meant to. We are going back to heathen times, it is true, but in those days when the foundation stone of any house, castle or bridge was laid, provision had to be made to give each its presiding, haunting, protecting spirit. Every great work began with sacrifice. Warlike expeditions began with an oblation of sorts. If a man was starting a journey he made an offering. A ship could not be launched without a sacrifice, and the breaking of a bottle of champagne on the bows of the ship in our own day is a relic of the breaking of the neck of a human victim and the suffusion of the prow with blood. Similarly, the burial of a bottle filled with coins under the foundation-stone is acceptable in these days and is a development of the ancient practice when human victims were used.

It is believed in some quarters that under the altars of some Christian churches a lamb was usually buried to impart security. This is an emblem of the true church lamb, the Saviour, who is the corner-stone of His Church. It was at one time thought that anyone who entered church at a time when there was no service was likely to see a little lamb spring across the choir stalls and vanish. This was believed to be the church lamb, and when this apparition appeared to anyone in the churchyard it was said to foretell the death of a child.

It was once the practice in Sussex to bury a bottle of pins under the hearthstone when a new house was being built, to protect it from witchcraft. There are many such substitutes for human sacrifices. From Germany we have the substitute of burying an empty coffin, or walling it up in a new structure, and it was a common belief that a lamb walled up under the altar would make a new church stand firm.

When the walls of old Delhi were being enlarged by King Alá-ud-din Khilji, AD 1269–1315, it is reported that the blood of thousands of goat-bearded Moghuls was mixed with the mortar. Before cement was used in building it was not uncommon for masons to mix mortar with the blood of oxen. While the blood doubtless had a hardening effect, it is likely that this practice in the first instance was associated with the superstition of foundation sacrifice.

In certain districts of Normandy this same substituted sacrifice survived as a house-custom well into the second half of the nineteenth century. It was believed that the tenant of a newly built house would die in the course of a year unless a cock was slaughtered and its blood poured on the threshold. When work began in 1892 on the Syrian Ottoman Railway, which was to connect Haifa with Damascus, an inaugural ceremony took place, at the cutting of the first sod. The Mussulman participation in the ceremony included the slaughter on the spot where the work was to begin of fifteen sheep, the blood from their throats being used to saturate the ground.

There was an old belief that when bridges were erected the work was accompanied by human sacrifice. It is perhaps from Wales that folklore has preserved the bridge-sacrifice tradition most clearly. There is a bridge called 'Devil's Bridge' near Beddgelert. Many of the people in that neighbourhood used to believe that this structure was formed by supernatural agency. It is said that the devil proposed to the neighbouring inhabitants that he would build them a bridge across the pass, on condition that, for his trouble, he should have the first to cross it. The bargain was made, and the bridge appeared in its place, but an old woman cheated the devil by whipping a dog in front of her. Here, of course, we have a substituted animal sacrifice for the original human sacrifice. Even in our time the laying of the foundation-stone of a famous building is often attended with ceremony; even though the sacrifice is no longer offered, the form remains. We are not even now completely free from the lingering remains of pagan superstition. When leaving one house for another, it was thought to be unlucky to move into a house which was too clean. Superstition claimed that all its good fortune got swept out with the dirt and was supplanted by evil. Thus grew up the custom of throwing a cat into a new house before its human occupants went in. Any evil spirit in the dwelling would take possession of the cat, which would soon sicken and die. Many tribes of the ancient American Indians especially the Karok, believed it unlucky to occupy the same wigwam a second time. It was thought that a deserted home was entered by malignant spirits who continued to live there. This may be compared with the parable found in the Christian gospel concerning the man who left his house 'swept and garnished', only to have it occupied by 'seven evil spirits'.

DOMESTIC CHORES

The idea of something uncanny being associated with the witch's cauldron has possibly developed from superstitions connected with a household's daily cooking. It was the practice in Shropshire that one person only should be allowed to stir the pot or put dough in the baking-oven. It was believed that if two persons shared this work it would cause strife in the house. On the other hand, each member of the family in turn was expected to stir the Christmas pudding. Popular belief maintained that, in order to keep away the witches, a cross should be placed on or over the bung-hole of every barrel, and a cross should mark every loaf baked for the household. In some parts of the country no baking was done where there was a corpse in the house, and a woman must never sing while she was baking the family bread. The bread baked at Christmas time was special in that it had to be baked during the night time, and the cakes were not to be counted by the cook. Nevertheless, a cake must be named for each person in the household, and if one should break during the baking, the person whose name was on it was believed to die before the following Christmas. Another baking adage runs: 'When making bread the cook must be sure to cross her fingers when adding the yeast else the witches will prevent her dough from rising.'

At Halesowen, Birmingham, many older women never throw dirty water down the sink on Good Friday. It is, instead, placed in a washing-tub, a dobie, and kept until the following day. It was believed that clothes washed on Good Friday would become spotted with blood; the origin for this being that, while Jesus was being led to Calvary, a woman who was washing by the wayside waved a dirty garment in his face. Then there was the washing jingle that ran through the week:

'They that wash Monday have all the week to dry,
They that wash Tuesday are pretty near by,

They that wash Wednesday make a good housewife,
They that wash Thursday must wash for their life,
They that wash Friday must wash in need,
They that wash Saturday are sluts indeed.'

As for the household chores upstairs, it is the actual staircase
that is the instrument of fortune, in this case, illfortune, for
superstition claims it is unlucky to pass anyone on the stairs.
This probably dates back to the Genesis story (Gen. 28.12) of
Jacob's dream of a ladder between heaven and earth, with
angels ascending and descending. The ladder was a symbol of
the means by which one could ascend to the gods, and it is
thought that the fear of treading on the same stair as a god,
and the possibility of incurring his wrath, is the reason for the
superstition. There is a way around this, however, since people
passing others on the stairs can always protect themselves by
crossing their fingers; and this, of course, refers to the protective
powers of the cross. Crossing one's fingers, indeed, is felt to
ward off many a disaster, and is an exact parallel to 'touching
wood'.

Many superstitions are a relic of man's primitive stage of
thought, when it was believed that all created beings existed
under the same conditions as man himself, subject to the same
desires and tribulations, and capable of the same feelings. Even
to this day in certain remote country districts pets, domestic
animals and bees are credited with an understanding of what
men say and do and are treated as members of the family who
own them.

In France on the Feast of the Purification it was usual in
some parts to read the gospel for the day to the inmates of the
hive, while in certain rural areas of France and Wales children
were told that if they used bad language within hearing distance
of the hive the bees would come out and sting them.

Connected with this belief in the quasi-humanity of bees is
the old custom that a hive or swarm must not be bought or
sold in case offence may be taken by the creatures. If they were
'exchanged for money' then it had to be gold, but more often
than not their value was measured by corn or hay, or some
other commodity which could be bartered.

After the death of the master of the house special notice was taken of the bees. If they swarmed it meant that they would not be happy with their new master, and should the swarm settle on a dead branch it was thought that the new master would not live very long. In the North of England bees were even thought to worship by humming the Hundredth Psalm in their hives. A death is, in some parts, reported to the bees, whereas in other areas it is told to the cattle or to the trees; and in some districts marriages and births are told to the bees. Well into the latter half of the nineteenth century it was not unusual to see hives draped with black crêpe when there was a death in the house, and this prevailed not only in every English county but in Normandy, Brittany, North Germany and Russia. It was believed that unless the bees were treated as members of the family they would either leave or die in their hives.

BIRDS AND THE BEES

Many children are still told that they were delivered by the birds and the bees, found under a gooseberry bush, or brought by a stork. 'A small girl who was told about the birds and the bees said she thought that if she were stung by a bee, she would have a baby.' Most children pick up garbled and wrong versions about birth, and the stork myth dies hard with parents since it is a convenient way of evading the 'Where did I come from?' plea which all children ask sooner or later. At one period christening tongs were favourite presents when a child was baptised. They were about the same size as an ordinary pair of sugar-tongs, but were cast in the form of a stork standing upright. When the tongs are opened for the purpose of lifting lumps of sugar the body, which is hollow, discloses the image of a baby in swaddling clothes. The practice of giving this kind of gift at baptism probably originated from the old Teutonic idea that newly born babies were brought by storks. The Dutch thought that a stork alighting on a housetop was a sign of happiness. To kill such a bird would be sacrilege.

It was at Godalming that one Mary Toft practised her strange deception, and managed to deceive not only the locals but also some learned men of the time. She pretended to have been delivered of several live rabbits, and Mr St Andre, surgeon and anatomist to the royal household, published a pamphlet in support of her assertions, with engravings of the rabbits, 'taken from life'.

Hogarth issued a satirical print to mark the occasion, entitled *Cunicularii, or the wise men of Godliman in Consultation*. The principal figures are St Andre and a Mr Howard, a surgeon of Guildford, who acted a prominent part on the occasion. St Andre was a quack, though he was no doubt deceived in this affair; but at least one physician of eminence in London supported Mary Toft's veracity, and the occurrence was so generally credited that it gave rise to the short-term custom of excluding rabbits from every dinner table.

A superstitious method of determining whether an unborn child would be male or female was to clean a mutton shoulder of every scrap of meat. The blade-bone was then held in the fire until it was scorched sufficiently to allow the thumbs to pass through the thinnest part. A string was passed through the holes thus made and, the ends having been knotted together, it was hung on a nail at the back door of the house last thing at night. The first person to enter the house in the morning, male or female, would bestow his or her sex on the expected child.

Primitive peoples believe that the moon is able to make women pregnant. The women of the Ahts and Greenlanders will still not look directly at the moon and will take care never to sleep on their backs without first rubbing spittle on their stomachs to prevent them swelling. Primitive people in Nigeria hold to the superstition that the Great Moon Mother sends a Moon Bird which brings the baby, and that a husband is not the vehicle of procreation. This belief is not unlike the myth of the stork.

The Malagasy believed that if a girl was born on a certain day, her first child was doomed to die. To avert this calamity, the child when she was old enough had to kill a grasshopper and wrap it in a specially made shroud. The dead insect represented her doomed child. She then caught more grasshoppers, pulled sufficient of their legs and wings off to prevent them flying away, and laid them around the corpse. The buzzing of the crippled insects represented the mourners at the funeral. The child then wept and mourned over the dead grasshopper, and after this it was thought that she would no longer have to fear for the life of her future baby, since the gods would not be so cruel as to make her mourn twice for a dead child.

The day on which a child was born was thought to influence its fortune as the years went on. Thus we have the old English verse:

> Monday's child is fair of face,
> Tuesday's child is full of grace,
> Wednesday's child is full of woe,
> Thursday's child has far to go,
> Friday's child is loving and giving,
> Saturday's child works hard for a living,
> But the child that is born on the Sabbath day,
> Is fair and wise, and good and gay.

Even to this day people will not allow a new pram into the house until the child has actually been born. In olden days it was a common superstition, held in places as far afield as the South of China, that if an empty cradle were rocked in a household where a new child was expected nothing but ill would befall the baby. Henderson records the superstition about rocking a cradle when it is 'toom' or empty.

NEWBORN

An unbaptised baby must never be left alone without some guardian talisman: a holy book, an article of the father's clothing, a knife or a sharp instrument. The first visit made by the mother after the birth of her baby was to be churched, a form of thanksgiving made by Christian women after giving birth. This practice was originally based on the Jewish rite of purification for women after childbirth which, according to Levitical law, demanded thirty-three days' observance for a male child and sixty-six days for a female (Lev. 12.5). In some parts of England it was not unlikely that a woman who had not been churched might receive insults and blows should she be seen out of doors before the ceremony.

Baptism, likewise, was regarded as urgently necessary for the child after its birth as was churching for its mother. If an infant had the misfortune to die before it was baptised, superstition decreed that its soul would enter a wild goose and be doomed until the Day of Judgement to wander earth-bound. A parallel belief held in Russia from ancient times claimed that 'will o' the wisp', a flame-like phosphorescence moving fitfully over marsh land, consisted of the spirits of stillborn babies.

To cry at its baptism was reckoned lucky for a child since, if it were quiet, the omen inferred that it was too good to live. This superstition probably arose from the practice of exorcism. When the devil was leaving a possessed person he usually cried out and rent the person severely; a screaming infant therefore at baptism was visible proof that the devil had departed.

Among primitive peoples a name was regarded as the private possession of the individual to be guarded at all times, since to know one's true name gave an enemy power to work bad magic against the owner. It was quite common for children to be given secret names which were known only to the family. The child usually possessed another name, a nickname. This was certainly the case among the tribes of the North American Indians, and it was also the practice among the ancient Egyptians and the Brahmins of India. Among the Eskimos it was thought that a change of name would ensure a change of luck in hunting or in affairs of the heart. This superstition rested on the belief that a change of name would bring about a change in the person. It is said that the early Christians changed their names when they were converted and baptised, but that they kept their Christian names secret from their pagan neighbours.

Another ancient superstition concerned with infants was that of deliberately not cutting their nails by artificial means until the child was a year old. To use scissors before his first birthday was thought to turn him into a thief. Thus, if a baby's nails grew uncomfortably long the mother had to bite them off. Then if the child's first nail-parings were buried in the roots of an ash tree, it was believed, the child would develop a good singing voice.

INITIATION

In some North American tribes a new-born son was prayed for to the Master of Life that he might be spared and grow. The ceremony consisted of boiling water with a sweet-scented root, some of which was first thrown into the fire and then distributed to the company present. When the child killed his

first animal a further ceremony was held, when one of the
senior members of the family would pray to the Great Spirit
to be generous to the lad and allow him to grow to be a great
hunter and in battle to take many scalps; and never to behave
like a woman! Their puberty rites for males included intro-
ducing the boy to the unseen world of spirits. The Omaha
brave, for example, at the age of fourteen was initiated during
a four-day ceremony of clay-daubing, tribal prayer-singing, and
fasting, when he met his patron spirit which would be his link
with the spirit world during his lifetime and would indicate
whether he was to be a medicine man, a hunter, or a warrior.

For the American Indian maid the puberty ritual was considered more important. Lasting from seven days to six months
in some tribes, it was a time of fasting, bathing, self-denial and
isolation. It was believed that whatever she did during the
period of her seclusion she would continue to do for the rest of
her life, the superstition being similar to that by which children
are told, even to this day, that what they do on their birthdays
they will do for the rest of the year.

Among ancient peoples, most notably the Jewish race, circumcision is one of the most important ceremonial rites observed. It was the practice in 3000 BC for the Egyptians to
circumcise boys between their sixth and fourteenth year, though
it is not certain whether it was extended to all males, or confined to the priestly caste and others who were connected in
some special way with the religious mysteries. In the great
majority of cases, however, circumcision was initiatory in
character, regarded as a preparation for sexual life, an effort to
avert sexual peril, a test of endurance, and a tribal mark
deemed necessary for the complete life of manhood. Originally,
circumcision was performed at the season of marriage, but with
the passage of time the rite was brought forward to the age of
puberty, and later still took place when a boy was between
three and five years old. Only Jews and Moslems carried out
the ceremony when the child was as young as one week. In
Egypt the boy was dressed as a girl to show that he belonged to
the weaker sex until after the rite was over. Among certain
tribes in Africa, however, it was in order to avert the attention
of evil spirits that boys were dressed as women at the period
of circumcision, to deceive the evil spirits into mistaking them

for girls and thus not injure them at this critical time. When the boys of the Masai in East Africa were circumcised, they were dressed in female garments and were actually made up as women, with painted lips and whitened faces. They continued to wear women's clothes until their wounds healed, after which they were regarded as men and were shaved for the first time and finally given all the paraphernalia of warriors.

The nearest approximation we have in the Western world to the puberty initiation is confirmation, when personal identity is believed to undergo a very real transformation. In the Church of England and among Lutherans and certain other Protestant groups a course of instruction in Christian faith and practice precedes confirmation, thus providing adolescents with a period of systematic instruction culminating in a religious rite.

MANY HAPPY RETURNS

Birthdays play a very vital part in superstition, The sign of the Crab or the year of the Cockerel will supposedly dictate one's character and fate! In the Western horoscope system it is believed that the sign of the zodiac under which a person is born, Aries, Taurus, Gemini, Cancer, Leo, Virgo, Libra, Scorpio, Sagittarius, Capricornus, Aquarius, or Pisces, will reveal a great deal about his personality. In Asia, the Chinese horoscope system relies upon dividing the years into groups of twelve, each of the twelve being given the sign or name of a chosen animal, always in the same order: Rat, Buffalo, Tiger, Cat, Dragon, Snake, Horse, Goat, Monkey, Cockerel, Dog and Boar. Should a person be born between 31 January 1957 and 15 February 1958, the year of the Cockerel, not only would he be inclined to strut but he would always have to scratch hard for a living.

Besides these popular superstitions, other birthday beliefs flourish. Thus, birthday greetings given to a child first thing in the morning were supposed to bring good fortune; and in Mexico, *mañanitas* (birthday songs), play an important part in the celebrations. Quite often a small orchestra is hired to pay this musical tribute and the musicians play for the day, and in order that the birthday songs shall be the first thing the person hears when he wakes, the music is played when the cock starts crowing, sometimes as early as two o'clock in the morning. Candles, too, are endowed with special power when used in birthday celebrations. If the birthday child makes a silent wish and then blows out all the candles in one puff that wish will be granted. Another superstition holds that each guest at a birthday celebration may make a silent personal wish and then blow out one of the candles only. Mystic significance has always been attached to lighted tapers and sacrificial fires. In some parts of Germany peasants used to light the birthday cake candles as soon as the child first awoke, and the candles were kept burning, being replaced as needed, until the cake was eaten by the family and guests. It was thought that if the candles were not kept burning then the child would not enjoy a happy year. Birthday wishes such as 'Happy Birthday' or 'Many Happy Returns of the Day' were thought to bring good fortune as long as they were given at the right time. As soon as the child awoke was considered the best time for greeting since this would ensure good fortune. Should the greetings arrive late, however, they were thought to bring bad luck.

Even in these days of hard realism and enlightenment, fragments of these old beliefs are still handed on to the rising generations, so that from the cradle with its songs and rhymes onwards, through infancy to childhood and bedtime stories, still further to the role of nursery school and kindergarten, mothers and teachers still share with small children that traditional folklore in which they themselves were nurtured.

CHAPTER FOUR

Faith and Worship

THE LINE dividing faith and superstition is a very thin one, and nowhere is its tenuity so clearly seen as in this aspect of religious superstition. The risks involved by established religions when they adapted a pagan practice to a hallowed framework were considerable, and their success was somewhat mixed. Such media as the dance, legendary heroism and sacrifice savoured of licentiousness, glamour and the macabre, which mixed very uneasily with a monotheistic religion whose root was morality, and whose substance was austere sobriety. Not that all dancing was abhorrent as a form of worship; nor was the incorporation of the classical heroes into Christian worship anything more than innocent; and as a general rule sacrifice was the highest form of revering the deity and beyond reproach. But there were exceptions. The fertility cult and the gruesome human and live sacrifices were inexcusably repugnant, and only with the passing of barbarism has their baseness been replaced with more acceptable reminders of the original principles.

THE CHRISTIAN TAKE-OVER

As the early patriarchs utilised the pagan symbols and practices around them for use in their worship of Yahweh, so, in time, did the Christian Church also. In primitive society the year is full of festivals, but none greater than that of the winter solstice which celebrates the apparent rescue of the sun from a total capture beneath the dark horizon. A new significance was given to the celebration of the winter solstice when the early Christian Church decided to commemorate Christ's birth at this time, which for thousands of years had been an occasion regarded with universal respect. The Church sought and succeeded in utilising the reverence surrounding the popular festivals which were essentially religious in origin, while purging the celebrations of the more profane practices of the pagans which had arisen, through the centuries, to obscure and alter the original character of the feast. The modern Christmas may be said to be a triumph of tolerance born of human understanding matured over centuries: it is the feast not only of man's redemption wrought by a holy child, but of man himself. It is the supreme feast of humankind since it releases, even if for only a short period, tendences which are repressed by the selfishness of mankind. Political and religious prejudices are shelved; tyrants show kindness; the poor are remembered; and all because it is Christmas.

With the advent of Christianity, the house-religion of the pagans, with its emphasis on the house altar and the sacredness of the threshold, was adapted to Church usage. Thus we find many of the religious rites surrounding the house-religion and its protection of the threshold being transferred from the house to the Church. An illustration of this prevailed in the village of Belford in Northumberland, where the bridal couple were made to leap over a stone placed in their path outside the church porch. This was called the petting stone, and marked the place where the bride, as she crossed it, must be rid of all her pettiness and humours.

A superstition akin to this was that grounded in the belief, in Great Britain and elsewhere, that the Deity was to be worshipped under the open sky. In spite of the fact that Churches were built and generation after generation passed away, this belief was so firmly rooted in the minds of people that provision had to be made in certain areas to worship out of doors near the churches. In Scotland, even down to the end of the eighteenth century, a sect existed called the Hill Folks who met on hills to perform their devotional exercises after the manner of their forebears. Train confirms this in maintaining in his *History of the Isle of Man*, that the mounds adjoining the churches in the island were used for the same purposes.

An obvious danger in this acknowledgement of superstition by the Christian Church was that it could cause confusion in the minds of uneducated people. The intention to hallow pagan customs with the Church's authority was not always clearly grasped, and people were left not at all certain of the boundary lines between faith and superstition. Thus, in the Christian catacombs, Pan and Orpheus appear as representing Christ the Saviour, and some of the epitaphs begin with the pagan address to the gods of the grave. Even the chair of St Peter was engraved with the labours of Hercules.

The Emperor Constantine 'was a superstitious man, and mixed up his Christian religion with all kinds of absurd superstitions and opinions' (Niebuhr). Even the coins of his reign carried on one face the letters of the name of Christ and on the other, the inscription *Sol invictus*, together with the figure of the sun-god. In the same way, Constantine stirred up confusion by retaining the old pagan name of *Dies Solis*, or 'Sunday', for the weekly Christian festival, so that the Christians among his subjects found themselves worshipping God on 'the venerable day of the Sun'. Another heresy connected with Sunday was the superstitious notion that people could be changed into stones for abusing the Lord's Day; and to confirm this common belief there can be seen in Cornwall a group of stones known as The Hurlers. These were believed to have been men once, who, for playing the game of hurling on a Sunday, were turned into stone. Similarly a stone group called The Nine Maidens were also believed once to have been young women who suffered the same fate for dancing on the Lord's day. There is a like parallel of this adoptive notion by Christianity of heathen practices in the intriguing custom among pagans of offering the first clippings of the beard to the deity. It was reckoned to be 'Christianised' when a priest made the same offering, but to God.

LORD OF THE DANCE

The dance would, nowadays, be considered a controversial means of offering thanks and praise to the deity, yet in the days of the Old Testament, when religion was still comparatively young, the dance, far from being frowned upon as irreverent, was in fact regarded as aptly symbolic of rejoicing; and amongst the Romans and Egyptians, the dance, in certain circumstances, was closely associated with religious ceremonies, as it was by David, second King of Israel, who himself led the dance on the return of the Ark of God from its long exile. In later Judaism also the dance survived in the religious celebration of the

Feast of Tabernacles. It is not unlikely that the dance was used by early Christians in order to express joy in the resurrection of the body. There was, however, a tendency for the free expression that dancing afforded to get out of hand and revert to the licentious nature of the pagan dance, so it became necessary to supress this particular form in which joy and thankfulness was expressed. Saint Augustine records with horror that dancers invaded the resting-place of Saint Cyprian at night and sang songs there. Pope Eugenius II (824–7) forbade dancing in churches. The Bishop of Orleans in 858 condemned the dancing of women in the presbytery on festivals, and the Council of Bayeux in 1300 condemned all dances which took place in church or in churchyards.

In primitive tribes, the dance has ever been used for veneration of the deities, and formed a major part of magico-religious functions. In early Semitic history the dance was a vital contributory factor to the frenzy and 'possession' necessary for function by the Baal prophets and the bands of the ecstatic *nebhiim*. A characteristic of the religious dance was the limping gait, and a clear example of this is given in the eighteenth chapter of the first book of Kings in the contest on Mount Carmel, when the prophets of Baal and Ashera 'limped about the altar they had made' in their attempts to bring down fire to consume the sacrifice.

Comparable with this is the solitary dance of the 'possessed' such as in the dance of the Maulawi dervishes in Pera, who move in circles to the accompaniment of music, and the circular dance performed by a group around an object set up for veneration. Songs sung while dancing in a ring penetrated into Christian worship at an early stage, but little is left of this superstitious practice save perhaps during the singing of Christmas carols, where traditionally the singers stand in a circle around a lantern. While some believe the word 'carol' is derived from the word 'chorus', others maintain that it comes from the debased Latin word 'corolla', meaning a ring or a small crown. It is perhaps significant that in olden times the word for a ring, or group, of stones such as those at Stonehenge was 'carol'. There is little doubt, however, that the earliest Christian carols were danced as well as sung.

In the civilised world, however, the dance has long since

ceased to be associated with religion; yet in time past and among primitive peoples, the dance was not only an expression of joy and thankfulness for benefits such as the sun or rain, but also a mode of prayer offered up for the attainment of desires.

For the Blackfeet Indians of North America the sun-dance was a great annual festival. Vows were made to the sun in times of danger and trouble, with accompanying offerings and prayers: 'The great Sun-god is our father,' said Mad Dog, the great orator of the Blackfeet, in dismissing the tribe when the sun-dance was over; 'he is kind, for he makes the trees to bud and the grass to become green in the springtime. He gave the people good hearts that they also might be kind and help each other' (MacClintock. *The Old North Trail*).

Even when preparing for the usual hunt, many North American tribes held magico-religious dances. As far as they were able they imitated their quarry in the hope of bringing the actual animal within range of their arrows. Catlin claims that every Mandan Indian was compelled by social law to keep a buffalo mask, made out of the skin and horns of a buffalo's head, in his lodge, in order to be ready to dress up for the buffalo dance to entreat the Great Spirit to send the Mandan villages a good supply of buffalo. During the dance, eight men, dressed in entire buffalo skins, imitated the appearance and movements of buffaloes, while four old men chanted prayers to the Great Spirit.

Very much akin to this is the purpose of the dance in primitive parts of Africa. Indeed, even when civilisation has sophisticated the old life, on special national occasions the old tribal dances are still revived; like the war dances performed in commemoration of brave deeds done by the warriors of time past. Equally integral are the fertility dances known among primitive societies throughout the world. The fundamental belief is that the crops of the earth can only flourish when blessed with a ritualistic dance simulating, or even enacting literally, union between the human sexes. The Baganda tribe of East Africa set great store by the efficacy of dances performed by the parents of twins. In connection with this superstition, a mother newly delivered of twins accompanies her husband round the district performing dances in the gardens of favoured neighbours, thereby promoting bumper plantain crops.

Imitative dances or pantomimes were indulged on the theory that the visual has greater power than the aural. Thus, it was believed that the unseen deities were more likely to take notice of bodily movements than to pay attention to the mere voice of a petitioner. It must have possessed great credibility, for when the Aht or Nootka Indians of Vancouver's Island danced the seal dance, they stripped naked, entered the water regardless of the nominal temperature and emerged presently dragging their bodies along the sand like seals, to crawl into their houses for the rescuscitating warmth of the fire, whence they would rush out presently and start dancing again.

Those who make their living by the sea are notoriously superstitious, and among the fishermen of the Torres Straits Islands dances were held from time to time to ensure successful fishing. Women were forbidden to enter any of the turtle-fishing canoes and were excluded from the company of the fishermen. The men anointed themselves with a mixture of turtle fat and wood-ash while their boats were purified by the smoke from burning herbs: images were put on board the canoes and their spirits were invoked by the crew to join them on their fishing expedition.

PRAYER

Any ritual observance that is performed in an attempt to bring man into a closer relationship with the unseen powers of nature may be said, in the broad sense, to be prayer; and this includes the dance as well as dramatic and symbolic ceremonies, and the spoken and chanted word. The secret and hidden character of prayer makes it difficult to assess its place in the daily lives of mankind through the ages, but there is evidence to support the claim that religious supplication is very deeply rooted in man.

In its simplest and most primitive form, prayer is the expression of a desire, which desire is asked of a power regarded as supernatural in the hope of prevailing upon that power to grant the request. With the development of monotheism prayer breaks into a new dimension, for to petition are added invocation and adoration. These facets of prayer Christianity has in common with the great world religions. Where Christian prayer transcends that of other beliefs is in its concept that prayer is a deep and militant fellowship between the soul and God, where all the lesser aspects of humanity become secondary to the prime purpose of prayer—consummation with the divine will. This prayer is offered 'in the name of Christ', whose mission, sacrifice, life, death and resurrection form the foundation and means whereby the Kingdom of God is established: that is by the defeat of evil and the perfecting of humanity.

Nevertheless, Tertullian (c. AD 160–c. 220) African Church Father, the first Christian theologian to write in Latin and to have created the language of Western theology, said of the most infidel nations, that 'nature in the midst of perils makes them speak with a Christian voice (*exclamant vocem naturaliter Christianam*) and have recourse to a God whom they invoke almost without knowing him' (*Ignoto Deo*). And Ragueneau said of the Huron Indians in 1648, 'Though they were barbarians, there remained in their hearts a secret idea of the Divinity and of a first Principle, the author of all things, whom they invoked, though they knew him not.'

It is recorded that among the Society Islanders there were religious rites which were connected with almost every act of their daily lives. 'An ubu or prayer was offered before they ate their food, planted their gardens, built their houses, launched their canoes, cast their nets, and commenced or concluded a journey' (Ellis. *Polynesian Researches*).

The Cape Monthly Magazine for July 1874 recorded how a Bushman was asked how he prayed to the god his tribe regarded as the creator of all things. In imploring tones he answered, 'O Cagan, O Cagan, are we not your children? Do you not see our hunger? Give us food!' 'And,' he concluded with artful naïvety, 'he gives us both hands full!'

Callaway in *The Religious System of the Amazulu* tells how the headman of a Zulu village sacrificed a bullock to the spirits of the dead, following the sacrifice with this prayer: 'I pray for cattle that they may fill this pen. I pray for corn that many people may come to this village of yours and make a noise and glorify you. I also ask for children, that this village may have a large population and that your name may never come to an end.'

Sometimes the interval between sacrifice and prayer was of considerable duration. Among the Ibo tribe of Nigeria, at the end of one year they offered to 'Aru' (the year) pots and clothes. These they heaped at the outskirts of the village, leaving them there entirely undisturbed until the year was over. It was only then that they actually called upon the power Aru asking him to relieve them of all pain and sickness and to grant them children. An unconscionable lapse between offering and petition perhaps, but requests for reasonable benefits nevertheless.

There are exceptions. Roman tradesmen, it seems, prayed to Mercury asking his assistance in defrauding their customers! Yet the rotten Roman Empire did not have the monopoly of perverted prayers. Quite apart from those which will thrive until the end of time, there is the quaint prayer of a clan of the Hervey Islanders in the South Pacific who, when bent on a thieving raid, artlessly besought Rongo, the Polynesian God of war:

'We are on a thieving expedition;
Be close to our left side to give aid.
Let all be wrapped in sleep;
Be as a lofty coco-nut tree to support us.'
(Gill. *Myths and Songs of the South Pacific*)

OFFERINGS AND SACRIFICE

As soon as man learned to believe in beings more powerful and wiser than himself, beings who controlled not only nature but the destiny of man, he gave himself to prayer and to the making of votive offerings. Man attributed consciousness to everything having life and force, and he had to distinguish between the helpful and the harmful, between food and poison, between benevolent spirits to be rewarded, and evil ones to be propitiated. It is little wonder that prayers and ceremonial rites for cleansing and protection, especially of the new-born, were common the world over. Among a tribe in the Fiji Islands when a child was born, it was the practice for its relations to make offerings to the priest who would pray: 'This is the food of the little child: take knowledge of it, ye Gods. Be kind to him. Do not pelt him or spit upon, or seize him, but let him live to plant sugar-cane.' The invocation for protection did not necessarily have to be offered in prayers. Amongst some East

African tribes it was tantamount to damning a child's growth altogether to indicate that child as 'so high', with the palm of one's hand facing the ground as though placed upon the child's head. Instead, to propitiate the spirits and retain their favour on the child, one indicated the child's height with one's hand vertical, thereby allowing for further growth.

Not all superstitions, however, were protective of children by any means; an integral part of ancient religious ceremonial involved human sacrifice. Acknowledged as the utmost limit of superstition, the offerings were frequently the young. Several passages of the Old Testament record the sacrifice of children to Molech, an ancient heathen god of one of the primitive tribes. 'Thou shalt not let any of thy seed pass through the fire to Molech' was the command to the Children of Israel (Lev. 18.21). Nevertheless there is unhappy evidence that, though only rare in Israel, human sacrifice was apparently recognised as legitimate until the time of the great ethical prophets. It is perhaps natural to ask here, if these prophets, inspired by God, taught that human sacrifice was abhorrent, why then should this same God choose this very death for his own son, and thereby seem to contradict himself?

The answer to this is vast and complex in the labyrinths it traverses to resolve this. A concise summary of Christian belief and teaching about the sacrifice of Jesus Christ and its purpose and relevance is made in the words of St John's gospel: 'God so loved the world, that he gave his only begotten Son, that whosoever believeth in him should not perish, but have everlasting life.' Thus the sacrificial death of Christ reconciled man with God.

There may, however, be those who will compare this sufficiency of the Christian sacrifice with that of the mystery religions; for since his death, there have been those who claim that the concept of salvation through Christ is exactly parallel to the central beliefs of the mystery religions. They equate Christ with Adonis of Greek mythology, with Attis, a male Asiatic deity, and with Osiris in the Egyptian pantheon who was pre-eminently the 'dead and resuscitated' god. Making this comparison, Loisy, writing in *The Hibbert Journal* in October 1911, says of Christ, 'He was a saviour-god, after the manner of Osiris, an Attis, a Mithra. Like them, he belonged by his

origin to the celestial world; like them, he made his appearance
on the earth; like them, he accomplished a work of universal
redemption, efficacious and typical; like Adonis, Osiris, and
Attis, he had died a violent death, and, like them, he had pre-
figured in his lot that of the human beings who should take
part in his worship, and commemorate his mystic enterprise;
like them, he had predestined, prepared, and assured the
salvation of those who became partners in his passion.'

To this the Christian would answer that the New Testament
sees Jesus as an historical person who, in loyalty to his Father's
purpose, suffered death on the cross, so that this death became
to men the pledge of the love of God and the forgiveness of sins.
The legends of the deaths of Osiris and Attis have nothing to
do with the purpose of spiritual redemption, and it is a cari-
cature to compare the legend of the murder of Osiris or the
self-destruction of Attis with the *self-sacrificing* death of Jesus.
In the mystery religions the death and restoration to life of
mythical divine persons is embodied in grotesque myths which
became the centre of an elaborate ritual, through which there
is conveyed to their votaries the hope of immortality. Those
who become followers of Christ dedicate their lives to his
obedience. This is not ritual; it is a new moral attitude to the
world and to God.

It must be admitted, however, that human sacrifice of
ordinary mortals was practised at one time or another, globally,
and even where it did not form part of the essential worship,
as in ancient Britain, evidence still exists to show that it did
at least occur in their history. Where human sacrifice pertained
it did not of necessity hold that the offerings were to be young.
According to the accounts of Caesar's Gallic Wars, the immortal gods regarded as equally acceptable the sacrifice, after
torture, of criminals. Should an appropriate number of such,
however, not be available, there were no scruples whatever in
subjecting the innocent, likewise, to such barbarity. Human
sacrifice must then have been widespread in Europe, for Caesar
goes on to write that 'The whole nation of the Gauls is much
addicted to religious observances, and, on that account, those
who are attacked by any of the more serious diseases, and those
who are involved in the dangers of warfare, either offer human
sacrifices or make a vow that they will offer them; and they

employ the Druids to officiate at these sacrifices; for they consider that the favour of the immortal gods cannot be con-
ciliated unless the life of one can be offered up for that of
another: they have also sacrifices of the same kind appointed
on behalf of the state. Some have images of enormous size, the
limbs of which they make of wickerwork and fill with living
men; setting them on fire, the men are destroyed by the
flames.' The Roman accounts of the sacrificial practices of the
ancient Druids, however, must be received with some suspicion.
There is the natural tendency for civilised communities to
exaggerate the horrors of superstitious observances amongst
remote nations, maintaining them to be barbarous. In one
sense, this is perfectly justifiable; the taking of human life can
never be dismissed lightly. Yet this early practice of sacrificing
human life to the gods arose from the belief that the nobler
the sacrifice, the more pleasing it would be to the gods. With
the humane and sophisticated qualities that civilisation brought
to people, however, the offering of human life to propitiate the
gods gave way to that of sacrificing animals instead. In the
beginning, it was customary to offer the whole animal. Only
as the ritual developed and became a fine art, did people prefer
to select certain parts of the beast as most efficacious. So it
became customary to burn only the legs and parts of the
intestines, while the remaining parts were consumed by the
people at a festive meal. It appears that the animals sacrificed
were usually of the domestic kind such as bulls, cows, sheep,
rams, lambs, goats and horses. The cock, however, is the
creature which has most commonly been associated with superstition. The ancient Greeks chose the cock and sacrificed it,
most often, to Apollo the god of medicine, or to his son
Aesculapius. The blood of a red cock was thought to possess
powerful medicinal properties, and in association with this
notion the burial of a live cock in the ground was not unusual
as a propitiatory offering. There may also have been some
special potency in the colour red, for it was a bird of this hue
that the Egyptians preferred for their offerings to Osiris—
possibly because this god was believed to have sprung from
the sun, and the sun's colour is closely akin to red. Red cocks
were significant in Irish history as well. There is reference made
to the sacrificing of nine of these birds, and the eve of St

Martin's Day and the festival of All Saints were favoured Christian occasions when such pagan sacrifice was used for their celebration.

The colour red may also have been significant for its easy association with blood. Blood, of course, plays a vast part in things religious and superstitious and, generally speaking, its pouring or sprinkling is its vital role. An interesting exception is found in Aztec superstition. The Aztecs believed that to spill even a drop of blood would incur savage vengeance from the gods. Consequently, every hunt they planned was preceded by an incense offering to the deities and concluded with a ceremonial smearing of their idol's face with the blood of the beast they had killed.

If blood is an integral part of sacrifice, then equally important is fire. No burnt offering could be made without it. It was this element which the Red Indians so peculiarly and concisely captured in what we now associate exclusively with their pattern of life—the pipe of peace. One scholar has defined it as 'The whole philosophy of burnt sacrifice contained in miniature'; but still possessing great power and meaning, for it was with the pipe of peace and the greeting 'There is peace between our peoples' that the two chiefs of the Huron and Iroquois tribes were reconciled after two hundred and seventy years of tribal bickering. Not only was the pipe smoked as a sign of peace; it was also used by braves preparing to cross a lake, to invoke the winds to be calm to ensure safe passage. There is another instance of the pipe being used as a propitiatory offering to the spirits of water: Brinton records that the Hurons used to offer tobacco to their local god and pray, 'Oki, thou who livest on this spot, we offer thee tobacco. Help us, save us from shipwreck. Defend us from our enemies. Give us good trade and bring us safe back to our villages.'

Shipwreck must remain till the end of time a constant fear of sailors. The possession of a cowl, the membrane sometimes covering the head of a child at birth, is a well-known charm amongst mariners as protection against such peril and much coveted by the superstitious among them.

In ancient times, Roman sailors who had been in danger of shipwreck and wished to humour the gods strung votive tablets in the temples and over the altars of the sea-god Neptune. In time, however, Neptune's authority waned in favour of the Egyptian goddess Isis; this was a curious development since Isis' own devotees in Egypt were known for their abhorrence of the sea and all things connected with it.

St Nicholas' Church in Liverpool, consecrated in 1361, is a concrete witness to the faith of British mariners in Providence. It appears that near it, once, was a statue of the patron saint, which statue (in an age when sailors had more faith in intercession of saints than in the seaworthiness of their craft) received incessant favours from those who went to and from their business in great waters.

WATER PURIFICATION

Deliverance from water then, was sought, and deliverance through it also. From being an element supposed to possess life in the days long before Christ, when spirits were believed to inhabit running water, it became a purifying element in the days of the Israelites in the wilderness when Aaron and his sons had their hands and feet washed with water as a means of purification 'Lest they die' (Exos 30.18-21). For the Christian at baptism, water was the 'outward sign of an inward invisible grace', and as such grew to be regarded by the time of the Reformation as an element holy in its own right. Holy water stoops were placed near church doors so that worshippers might, as they went into church, dip the fingers of their right hand into the water and bless themselves with the sign of the cross. The making of holy water could be effected by the addition of salt, first exorcised, blessed, and then thrown into the water *in modum crucis*, when a further blessing was recited over the two elements thus mixed. Such properties associated with holy water and especially with water consecrated for Holy Baptism, however, were open to abuse. Thus in 1236 the Archbishop of Canterbury was obliged to order that fonts were to be kept locked under seal, because the hallowed water used in baptism was frequently stolen for superstitious and magical purposes. In the Middle Ages the consecration of the water for baptism involved a lengthy ritual, including the symbolic acts of floating oil over the surface of the water in the form of a cross and plunging in two lighted tapers, performed by a bishop. The water thus hallowed remained in the font for a long time; which fact necessitated a clause in Cranmer's first English Prayer Book of 1549, that 'the water in the Fonte shall be chaunged every moneth once at the least.'

It is easy to see how the actual hallowed element, water set apart by the Church, became coveted for superstitious misuse; just as vulnerable, however, was the actual performance of washing. The very fact that it was a holy rite exposed it to the evil medium of sorcery. So washing, or cleanliness and purification, plays an enormous part in taboo. In primitive society it is taken to seemingly obsessional lengths. One basic cause for this stipulation was the obvious belief that the agent had to be clean before he approached things sacred, lest he contaminate them; but the reverse was also true; contact with sacred objects must not be passed on indiscriminately. To touch a sacred object signified the necessity to wash, and even change one's clothes as well sometimes. So the Greeks believed that after sacrificing they had to wash both body and clothes (in a river) before returning home. In the same way, a Jew had to wash his hands after reading the Scriptures, and the priests, the descendants of the cohenüm have their hands washed even now before they ascend the rostrum in the synagogue to recite in a special cantilation the priestly benediction.

SACRED AND UNCLEAN

The sacred object was not of necessity a conventionally hallowed thing; to some peoples the pig was sacrosanct, and therefore these same principles of washing and changing were demanded. Animals, of course, have ever been regarded as sacred agents in the realm of superstition. In ancient Egypt the goose was an object of adoration in the temple. Then certain animals were regarded as sacred to certain deities: the panther and dragon to Bacchus; the crow and the wolf to Apollo; the stag to Diana; the deer to Hercules; the eagle to Jupiter; the horse and the vulture to Mars; the cock to Mercury; the dove to Venus. On the same basis it was thought in the Middle Ages that the devil and all his angels claimed the dragon, the swine and the serpent. Plutarch maintained that 'the Egyptians worship God symbolically in the crocodile, for being the only animal without a tongue, it is like the Divine Logos, which standeth not in need of speech.' Certainly the crocodile was regarded as a symbol of deity among the Egyptians.

A curious side issue in the matter of 'sacred beasts' was the fact that some of these creatures were eaten in the belief that their characteristic qualities would thereby be imparted to their eaters. As one would expect, therefore, to eat the flesh or drink the blood of lions was thought by some peoples to pass on courage. Their sacred goose, the ancient Egyptians believed, would, if eaten, give them its mental vigour. By the same reasoning, creatures like the hare or deer were to be avoided, since to eat their flesh would be to take into oneself their traits of timidity.

One of the most widely known food taboos is that of the Jews where 'unclean' animals are concerned. Among the ancient Jews it was considered lawful to eat those animals which chewed the cud and had parted hoofs; but only those fish which had fins and scales were considered clean, and birds of prey were not to be eaten on any account. On the issue of pigs, Frazer offers this interesting evidence: 'The Jewish attitude towards the pig was ambiguous,' and it could not be determined whether they 'worshipped or abominated' it. So they were not allowed to eat it, nor yet, it seems, to kill it. Thus swine were both unclean and sacred at the same time. There is support for the latter theory in the evidence we have that down to the eighth century BC Jews were known to meet secretly to 'eat the flesh of swine and mice as a religious rite'.

In consideration of purification rites, it is relevant to take account of the significance of colour. As one might imagine, white is the colour associated with purity and innocence; thus white was the colour worn by the ancient Druids, and was the colour appropriate to the priesthood in ancient times as well as today. This notion extended to cover white in general, even to white oxen being chosen as sacrificial offerings in the Druidic rites, or white horses at one time being the particular choice for sun sacrifice. In Spain white elephants, though not sacrificed, were considered sacred. In England today, or at least at the turn of the century, a white horse was a sign for good fortune and the reaction at seeing it was to 'spit for luck'.

RIGHT AND LEFT

Very significant in superstitious ritual is the distinction between right and left. Thus the practice of holding the chin or the forehead with the right hand during worship seems to have had its origin in superstition. The taking of the left thumb in the right hand in time past was employed as a remedy, but to cross one's legs or intertwine the fingers was regarded as a malevolent charm. Many people still pay strict observance to right and left, especially when dressing first thing in the morning. It was a Jewish practice to put on the left stocking and the right shoe first without tying it; then afterwards to put on the left shoe and then complete dressing with attention to the right side, which was considered to be the more fortunate. Even bishops were not excluded from this notion by the very superstitious: should a bishop confirm with his right hand, all was well; but to use his left hand was to initiate all kinds of misfortune on the unfortunate candidate. Confirmation was believed by some to be as good for rheumatism as it was necessary for initiating Anglicans into full church membership, and the superstition was that the oftener you could get yourself confirmed the more surely you would gain relief from the rheumatic scourge. Such was the power and validity of the bishop's right hand!

Fundamental as an element in matters of superstition was the word, just as it is, of course, throughout life. When conjurers and entertainers use the words 'hocus pocus' to catch the attention of the audience when performing a trick the words they use are a degeneration (originally intended as a parody, dating from the seventeenth century) of *Hoc est corpus* from the Latin Mass. As the words of prayers degenerate to magician's pass words, in the same way prayers offered by ignorant and uneducated people were couched in degenerate words. One such prayer was as follows:

> 'From witches and wizards and long-tail'd buzzards,
> And creeping things that run in hedge-bottoms,
> Good Lord, deliver us.'

CHAPTER FIVE

Evil and Wickedness

As SUPERSTITION can be sanctified by Christian redirection, so it can be appropriated by sorcerers and put to evil, demonic purposes; and it is ironic that the generation of the latter twentieth century, who smile patronisingly at their artless ancestors because of their fears of hobgoblins and haunted churchyards, are themselves once again becoming enthralled by the evil element in the supernatural. Unclean and sacred beasts, human transformation into animals, vampires and werewolves, wax effigies and the evil eye are but a short step from witches and devil-worship. And if the Middle Ages were rife with such wickedness, it was no less matched by the evil which succeeded it in the persecution of supposed witches and the superstitious means by which folk sought protection from them and the malefic power they possessed.

DREAD OF EVIL
'Witchcraft in Wales'
'Following a minor outbreak of black magic in the Principality, the Archbishop of Wales has called for co-operation from his clergy. Devil-worship—usually taking the form of the Black Mass—has been reported in Monmouthshire, Flintshire and other parts of Wales. In an effort to learn more about such cases, the Archbishop has asked his bishops and clergy to find out the extent of witchcraft practised by intruders who break into churches.'

This quotation was not found in a book from the Middle Ages, but was a press clipping of the early seventies of the twentieth century. Thus, there still survive among civilised people ideas and practices corresponding to those found in the various stages of development of primitive man. The belief in, the fascination by, and the dread of evil spirits underlie many superstitious practices, and as it is one of the earliest beliefs of the human mind, so it is one of the most persistent. There was a time when the whole world was thought to be overrun with apparitions, boggles, bloody-bones, bug-bears, black dogs, brownies, barquests, break-necks, boggy-boes, demons, dobbys, fairies, fantasms, fetches, ghosts, ghouls, goblins, hags, hob-goblins, hobhoulards, hobthrusts, ignesfatui, jemmy-burties, kelpies, mumpokers, night-bats, Robin-goodfellows, scrags, spirits, spectres, spellycoats, scarecrows, vampires, witches, warlocks, wizards; and there was not a single community but had its particular evil spirit. All the churchyards were haunted; every old house or ruin had its spectre; all the lanes had their guardian apparitions; every village common had its circle of fairies; and there was hardly a person who had not seen a spirit.

It would be wrong to suppose that such beliefs were limited to people living in remote rural areas. The superstitions of miners in former days were many and terrible, perhaps the most sinister being the fear of the knockers, whom they believed to be ghosts sentenced to work endlessly at knocking and picking the coal. Charles Kingsley, in *Yeast: A Problem*, 1851, recorded the superstition prevalent among Cornish miners in the 1830s that, 'They are the ghosts, the miners hold, of the old Jews, sir, that crucified our Lord, and were sent for slaves by the Roman emperors to work the mines; and we find their old smelting-houses, which we call Jews' houses, and their blocks of tin, at the bottom of the great bogs, which we call Jews' tin: and there's a town among us, too, which we call Market-Jew—but the old name was Marazion, that means the Bitterness of Zion, they tell me.' 'And bitter work it was for them, no doubt, poor souls!'

To this day some superstitious people believe fairies to be spirits which once inhabited human bodies but in some way have become earthbound. It was a general Irish superstition that 'the good people', as the fairies were called, often took a child from its parents, substituting a fairy for it. In Scotland it was once believed that a new-born child was under the spell of the fairies until it sneezed; then, and only then was the danger passed. So seriously was this superstition taken that midwives would occasionally take a pinch of snuff to make the new-born child sneeze, then a finger was drawn across its forehead as if to make the sign of the cross accompanied by rejoicing that the child was not a warlock. Among the ancient Welsh bards it was the end of life that was most feared, since they believed that the souls of Druids, who were not good enough to go to heaven yet not wicked enough to be damned, wandered the earth until the judgement day when they would be admitted to a higher state.

The dread of evil spirits by man has also been attributed to animals. It is not unknown for horses, dogs, and other animals in close relationship with man to refuse to take a certain path, as if they sensed danger or evil of some sort. There is scriptural warrant for this concerning the refusal of Balaam's ass to go forward, even when urged by the prophet. Certain of God's creatures have always been associated with good and evil: the dove is a universal sign of purity and was regarded as a holy bird in many religions, including Christianity, and the lamb, signifying innocence, was regarded as a symbol of Christ himself. It was at one time believed that witches could transform themselves into any creatures except a dove or a lamb, and even plain spoken non-superstitious people of today will innocently maintain that to see the first lamb of the season with its head towards you is a lucky omen. A black lamb, however, was considered to bear the devil's mark and likely to bring misfortune. The devil's mark was also thought to be carried by pigs in the form of six small rings on the inside of each foreleg, said to have been caused by the devil's fingers when he entered the herd of swine which 'rushed down a steep place into the sea'. (Mark 5.13). The Jews classed the ferret, the frog, the chameleon, the lizard, the mole, and the snail as unclean and thought them to possess demonic qualities. The creature thought to be held in greatest favour by Satan, however, was the cat, and it was not uncommon for inhabitants of ancient Egypt to shave their eyebrows upon losing a cat by natural death. During the Middle Ages, the cat was especially regarded as a creature or familiar of witches, and it is likely that superstitions regarding demonic creatures were derived from the ancient religions. Beelzebub, the Lord of the Flies, was a deity recognised by the ancients and worshipped in the form of a fly, and when the festival in honour of Apollo was celebrated in ancient Greece, an ox was sacrificed to the flies. When, in 1679, the Archbishop of St Andrew's was murdered, upon the opening of his tobacco box a living humming bee flew out, and that was at the time thought to be a familiar or devil.

The belief that human beings could from time to time be transformed into animals was not uncommon. Thus the fantasy prevailed that young maidens could transform themselves into hares, which could only be shot with silver sixpences. Many a white hunter in Africa has been prevented from shooting monkeys, since they were looked upon as men transformed for their evil deeds. In Abyssinia it was thought that miners could change themselves into hyaenas, and there was a time when the Portuguese peasantry believed that if a woman was delivered of seven male children successively, the seventh became subject to the powers of darkness, and every Saturday evening assumed the likeness of an ass. It was a widely held medieval European superstition that certain men could turn themselves into wolves, which could not be killed by any weapon unless it had been blessed and dedicated to St Hubert. The werewolf would roam at night devouring children and recently buried corpses.

BLOODSUCKERS

Perhaps the most sinister development in this class of superstition was belief in vampires. A vampire was thought to be the dead body of a criminal or heretic which continued to live in some mysterious way when in the grave, which, however, it was thought to leave at night in the form of a bat in order to suck blood from the living. Consequently, the body of a vampire was believed to remain in good condition instead of becoming decomposed like normal dead bodies. The bite of a vampire was regarded as fatal, and life could only be prolonged and the victim be protected from a second visit from the vampire by eating some earth from the grave of a vampire and smearing himself with his blood. Sooner or later, however, the victim died, was buried, and himself began a vampire life from the grave, nourishing his own body and infecting others with vampirism.

This superstition survived into the second half of the nineteenth century in Eastern Europe, where at the beginning of the eighteenth century it spread like a pestilence through Serbia and Wallachia bringing death and fear in its wake. Herbert Mayo records the remarks of Erasmus Francisci on the description of the Dukedom of Krain by Valvasor: he speaks of a man named Grando, in the district of Kring, who died, was buried, and became a vampire, and as such was exhumed for the purpose of having a stake thrust through him. 'When they opened his grave, after he had been long buried, his face was found with a colour, and his features made natural sorts of movements, as if the dead man smiled. He even opened his mouth as if he would inhale fresh air. They held the crucifix before him, and called in a loud voice, "See, this is Jesus Christ who redeemed your soul from hell, and died for you." After the sound had acted on his organs of hearing, and he had connected perhaps some ideas with it, tears began to flow from the dead man's eyes. Finally, when after a short prayer for his poor soul, they proceeded to hack off his head, the corpse uttered a screech, and turned and rolled just as if it had been alive—and the grave was full of blood.'

EYE-FASCINATION

Far more universal was the superstitious belief in the fascination caused by eyes. Just as birds are attracted to the jaws of a serpent, so in some animals the power of eye-fascination is irresistible. It is thought that certain species of fish, when they approach the surface of the sea, remain almost paralysed until the sea birds their enemies, flying overhead, dive and make a meal of them. And it is a common belief even to this day that a tiger or a lion on meeting the continued stare of a human being will cringe and never attack. From the beginning of time power for good or evil has been attributed to the eye. When eyes were painted on a Sinhalese image, for example, what was a lump of clay or a piece of stone became a 'god'. A godparent looking into the water in the font during a baptism is said to make the child grow up in the likeness of the godparent, and at one time it was believed that some men could even cause pregnancy in women simply by a sideways glance of the eye.

Belief in the supposedly terrible effects of the evil eye, which plagued so many countries and all classes among the Moslems, Hindus, and Oriental races, is one of the chief survivals of witchcraft. The witches' colour was thought to be red since it was symbolic of the blood with which they sealed their compacts, and is used in connection with witchcraft and charms throughout the world. Protective charms against the evil eye in Italy and Sicily were usually made of red coral and were tied with red woollen braid. Belief in the power of the evil eye persisted longer in Italy than in any other country in Europe. Indeed, the superstition was so strong in Sicily and south of Rome that the peasants would cross their thumbs with their forefingers if a hunchback crossed their path or if they met a person with a squint. This superstition was rampant centuries ago in almost every European country, and the 'gobbo' or hunchback, while being credited with the power of casting the evil eye, was also thought to be a protection against its effects if the hump on his back was touched. Superstition exists among all classes of society in all parts of the world, and belief in witchcraft still exists to this day. Certain individuals are thought to have the power to cast spells or make curses which will produce some evil effect on any object, animate or inanimate, so long as they are able to command the necessary supernatural power, which is usually acquired as a result of a compact made with the devil and sealed with the witch's own blood.

WITCHCRAFT

Directions for becoming a witch vary in different areas, but it was at one time believed in Cornwall that if any man or woman desired to enter into a bargain with Satan for the purpose of gaining the evil powers of witchcraft, that person went to Communion to receive the Blessed Sacrament; instead of consuming it, however, it was to be concealed and carried away. At midnight this stolen host was to be carried three times around the church, its bearer circling to the left, and it was believed that at the completion of the third lap the person would meet a huge toad crouching open-mouthed. If the sacrament was given to this creature, it would breathe twice upon the giver and he or she would at once become a witch or a warlock.

There have been records of Christians renouncing their faith to become followers of Satan and carry his mark. The form was that the proselyte renounced her baptism and gave herself over to the devil, soul and body, putting one hand on the crown of her head, and the other to the sole of her foot. It was thought that this caused the name of the proselyte to be erased from the Book of Life and inscribed in the blackest book of death. The satanic mark was thought to be a spot of any kind on the body, occasionally taking the form of a hare's foot, a lizard, or a toad.

A form of witchcraft which has been practised for thousands of years throughout the world, among primitive and civilised peoples alike, consists in the making of a wax figure in human shape, in order to injure or destroy an enemy. These wax effigies were used in the worship of the god Amen Ra in ancient Egypt in the great temple at Thebes. The practice passed over to Greece and from there to Rome, and in early times this practice was introduced into western Europe. The same form of magic can be traced in the far East. After the figure had been moulded in human form it was the practice to pierce it with pins. In England, the Lord's prayer was then repeated backwards, and prayers were made to the devil that he would inflict on the person whom the figure represented pains in the parts pierced with the pins. A variation of this was to use the heart of an animal, since the heart was regarded as being the source of life. The heart was given the name of the person the witchcraft was supposed to injure, and then stuck with sharp thorns or pins or twigs of witch hazel along with incantations, and it was thought that the person whom it was wished to injure would suffer in a similar manner. Recorded instances of magic used by witch-doctors in Africa are legion. One such, recording evil magic used against a European official by a Nigerian witch-doctor, described the ju-ju as being a fetish comprised of eight human skulls, four human thigh-bones, a dagger and an iron skewer, and a hand carved in wood. It was believed that the evil was to be directed against a European official because pieces of paper found under one of the human skulls were torn from government documents.

The imitation of sanctified acts is not unusual in superstitions, but one of the darker sides of medieval superstitions was the perversion of holy things in witchcraft. It was believed that spiritual power could be used either for good or ill. A written charm, hidden under an altar so that the priest would unknowingly say Mass over it, was thought to endow the charm with spiritual power which could afterwards be used against a victim. A more sinister practice was the use of the Mass for the Dead in the name of the living person said by a renegade or unfrocked priest; no changes were made in the service itself but only in the intention. It was also thought that the consecrated Host, if stolen or in some way removed from the church, would endow a thief with supernatural powers, and it was also used in some of the more sinister forms of black magic. Even to this day the recommended number for a coven in Britain is thirteen, the original number adopted by witches for their covens in mockery of our Lord and his Apostles.

A great many people at our modern breakfast-tables practise the old superstition of breaking the upturned shell of a boiled egg which they have eaten. Originally, according to Sir Thomas Browne, 'the intent thereof was to prevent witchcraft; for lest witches should draw or prick their names therein, and veneficiously mischief their persons, they broke the shell'. Others believed that witches could make use of an eggshell which was at least half perfect as a boat in which they could fly or sail away to other regions. Witches were believed to be able to transport themselves through the air powered by the devil. 'They go sometimes on a goat, sometimes on a horse, and sometimes on a broom, and generally leave their house by the chimney' (Boguet). It was generally believed that witches anointed themselves with magical ointment, prepared from the most gruesome ingredients before taking flight, which flight, most ancient sources claim, the witch carried out completely naked. It is recorded that the fat of a dead red-haired person was in demand centuries ago as an ingredient for poisons and potions used in witchcraft.

WITCH-HUNTING

The superstition of witchcraft stretches back into remote antiquity and has many sources. In Europe it was partly of Druidical origin, coming mainly from the Celtic areas of Britain, France and Spain. The Druidesses, called 'allrune' (all-knowing), were part priestesses and part old women who dabbled in magic and medicine. The main source, however, from which this superstition derived was the East, and the traditions and facts recorded in the Old Testament. From the beginning of medieval times until the fourteenth century, the devil had been treated as a somewhat ridiculous figure. He was regarded in fact as being full of trickery, malice, and naughtiness, yet impotent, stupid, and easily frustrated by the sign of the cross, a prayer, a sprinkling of holy water, or by the presence of a sacred relic. After the Black Death people began to take the devil more seriously, and demonology tended to compete with theology as a subject for study and meditation. During the fourteenth century the horrors of hell and the perils of being possessed by evil spirits became the subject of more and more sermons. Terrifying pictures were painted for the people depicting the tortures of the damned, not only in word form but actually painted on the walls of churches. The most appalling development was the increasing belief in witchcraft and the persecution of suspected witches which followed it during the fifteenth and sixteenth and seventeenth centuries. The ferment of thought, the ignorance, and the enthusiastic faith of the common people only needed the papal bull issued by Innocent VIII, ordering that all inquisitors should be vigilant and merciless in searching out persons suspected of witchcraft, to set fearful people on a road of torture and burnings which claimed more than one hundred thousand victims in Europe. In France and Germany especially, thousands of unfortunate people were slaughtered in the ensuing two centuries. It is recorded that many districts and large towns burnt two, three, and four hundred witches every year, and that in some the annual persecutions destroyed nearly one per cent of the whole population. It was not until the beginning of the seventeenth century that the superstitious fear of witches took on a crusading attitude in England. It is estimated that some 40,000 persons were put to death in that century in England alone. So great was the popular superstitious belief in the fatal powers of witches that, when preaching before Queen Elizabeth I in 1558, Bishop Jewel said, 'It may please your grace to understand that witches and sorcerers are marvellously increased within your grace's realm! Your grace's subjects pine away even unto the death, their colour fadeth, their flesh rotteth, their speech is silenced, their senses are bereft. I pray God they never practise further than on the subject.' He maintained that to put witches to death was to be obedient to Holy Scripture. At this time an old crazed priest who was nearly eighty years of age and had been a minister for fifty years was accused of dealings with the devil. Baxter reports on this incident as follows:

> 'Among the rest an old reading parson named Lewis, not far from Framlingham, was one that was hanged, who confessed that he had two imps, and that one was always helping him in doing mischief and (being near the sea) as he saw a ship under sail, it moved him to sink the ship, and he consented, and saw the ship sink before him.'

The old Saxon method of trying culprits by water was renewed in Britain in order to examine witches. It is recorded that the Reverend John Lewis did not sink when he was ducked in Framlingham moat and that one of his parishioners, John Rivett, claimed that this test was 'no true rule to try him by, for they put in honest people at the same time, and they swam as well as he'.

Six general symptoms were said to depict demonic possession: discordant screams, a distorted and horrible visage, numbness of the limbs, restlessness, unnatural strength and personal suffering. Speaking in an untaught language was, in time past, considered to be infallible proof of demonic possession, since demons were thought to be universal linguists, and to avoid detection they adopted the vernacular tongue even though they have no proper language of their own. It was thought in testing for demonic possession that a witch was unable to repeat the Lord's prayer and unable to shed tears. Torture was not uncommon in the detection of witches, and it is interesting that consecrated salt and herbs blessed by a priest were often used in the torture-chamber to protect those supposedly seeking out the evil; and even their instruments of torture, in some instances, bore three tiny marks representing the protective power of the Trinity.

EVIL REPELLENTS

Protection from evil spirits in general and witches in particular has always occupied the mind of man. All over the world there has been a high regard for things red: the berries of the rowan and thorn; the breast of a robin; the predilection for red feathers in the islands of the Pacific; the use of red in the Christian Church as the colour to denote martyrdom— believing it to be a strong repellent to witchcraft. One of the commonest safeguards against evil spirits in China was a red thread tied to some part of the body, just as in olden days in England a red silk tied round a finger was thought to ward off the power of witches. Among trees the rowan and the yew were believed to be specially effective against witchcraft. Rowan branches were tied together with red thread and hung over houses and barn doors in order to protect them from evil, and it was perhaps due to the fact that yew had such a close connection with sacred things, that it was thought especially hateful to witches, and that any place sheltered by it was safe from their influence. Other recipes for witchcraft prevention were less palatable. 'Take out the heart of a fresh-caught mole before it has ceased to beat, and eat it at once. This will act as an insurance against witches and the evil chance of all kinds.' Or again, 'Throw a handful of salt on the road, and place a knife near. If the witch passes she will cut her feet, while other folk will go unharmed.' The giving of coral to a baby girl at baptism by the godparents is still a fairly general practice. In olden days coral was thought to ward off the evil eye, and closely associated with this custom was the use of dill, which was regarded as a deterrent to witches and evil spirits. Dill water, in fact, is used to this day, especially in rural areas, when the baby is troubled with wind or teething.

At baptisms and communion services in some churches a small door set into the north wall used to be opened 'to let the devil out,' for the notion prevailed that the devil lurked on the north side of the church to claim the innocent and unwary.

According to one superstition, if you met the devil, you should either cut him in half with a straw, or force him to disappear by spitting over his horns.

The Christian Church has recognised five different methods of expelling demons: calling on the name of Christ; the use of relics; by the sign of the cross; by consecrated things, and by exorcism and adjuring the demon. Holy water, consecrated wax, and the *clangor campanarum* were considered to be the most effective methods of exorcism.

While the practice of exorcism was commonplace in medieval times, recorded instances of the superstitious practice of 'cursing by bell, book and candle' are quite rare. Ingham records that, 'A document, dated 31st October, 1442, is a commission and mandate from the Archdeacon of Chester, in Latin, addressed to all the chaplains and clergy within the archdeaconry, commending them to admonish three times, and peremptorily, "all those sons of iniquity",' who had poached the water of, or stolen from, the Worshipful Thomas de Legh, of Norwood. 'And if these evildoers did not, within fifteen days of each monition, make full satisfaction and restitution, then they were to be openly and publicly excommunicated "With bells rung and candles lighted, and the cross in the hands upraised" and all other legal solemnity' (*Cheshire: Its Traditions and History*).

The superstitious belief in maledictions was supported by passages in the scripture which stated that, in resentment at an offending prophet, Jeroboam 'stretched out his hand from the altar, saying, Lay hold of him. And his hand, which he stretched out against him, dried up, so that he could not draw it back to himself' (1 Kings 13:4). From time to time oblations made in churches owed more to superstition than to the Christian faith. The Welsh *Offrwm Gelyn*, the offering of one's enemies, is perhaps closest to the custom of calling down maledictions in the ancient world. In this weird rite a man, imagining himself injured or aggrieved, went to a church dedicated in the name of some famous and powerful saint; and there, kneeling upon his bare knees, and first propitiating the saint with an offering of money, he called down every conceivable malediction upon the head of his supposed enemy, his family, possessions, and descendants.

CHAPTER SIX

Luck, Good and Bad

EVERYONE, IT seems, from cavemen, tribesmen, and peasants, to patriarchs, presidents and prelates, the love-lorn, the childless, the rich, the poor, filmstars and housewives, sportsmen and flower-children, students, entertainers, farmers and city folk, all of us are gamblers when it comes to Lady Luck and her powerful charm. Luck charms spread their influence far and wide so that fortune or ill is kept or avoided by things carried, possessed, or even seen or acted out. Some are traditionally accepted symbols of luck, such as wood, salt, iron and the cross. Many, however, have no traditional roots, like a favourite dress or tie, an unlucky number or journey. Still other talismans are worn symbolically, though their origins are lost in time. Thus married women and bishops wear rings, and the military have their badges and insignia.

The loose meaning of the term amulet or fetish indicates protection or good fortune: it is known nonetheless to include more sinister powers like black magic or the voodoo of Africa, and to have upheld or destroyed the morale of nations. It is comforting to reflect that its most common significance nowadays is light-hearted, and except among a minority of serious devotees it is regarded as a quaint eccentricity.

PROTECTIVE DEVICES

In spite of the deletion of St Christopher in the Calendarium Romanum, published by order of Pope Paul VI in 1969, nullifying the efficacy of Christopher as a saint, St Christopher medallions are still carried by trusty enthusiasts. In the latter part of the twentieth century there has also been an epidemic growth in the popularity of the crucifix as well. Strung on a fine chain and worn around the neck, these crosses are believed to protect the wearer from bad luck in the same way as any other talisman or amulet.

It must be said immediately, however, that although these two devices have quite obvious connections with religious belief, the disposition of their devotees, can well be described as 'liberal' since many wear such trinkets as charms of protection rather than as symbols of devotion to their god. Thus, while the roots of the safeguard are grounded in faith, the attitude of their wearers may generally be described as nothing more than a wish for protection from bad luck, or even simply blind superstition; and it may be said without doubt or misinterpretation that there is a vast difference between the religious vitality of these and that of Joan of Arc when she asked for a cross to hold in her hands when she was burnt at the stake.

Trust in charms, however, has persisted from time immemorial; long before Christianity and its Church came into being and had its own signs added. The basic name for these charms was 'amulet', deriving from the Arabic verb *hamala* to carry, and covered a wide variety of emblems from flints, moon crescents, and stones with naturally worn holes right through them to that highly prized 'energiser' the mandrake plant. Over the years others joined them so that good luck symbols now include jewels, four-leafed clovers, crooked sixpences, lucky pigs, beads, bells, heather, horseshoes and the charm beloved of children, the rabbit's foot.

Obviously, these protective symbols—or fetishes—were taken more seriously in a primitive society: (indeed, the contemporary meaning of the word 'fetish' to denote an obsession gives some indication of the fanatical quality of the trust placed in it). Sprung from the word for 'amulet', and used by early Portuguese sailors in connection with West African tribesmen's charms of safekeeping, the fetish became used to cover almost every kind of venerated object, and was thought by the believer to act as a guardian of life and property and to give warning of misfortune. It was also, indeed, employed to bring down punishment on enemies. Thus in those early days the powers of the fetish had to be renewed occasionally with libations of blood.

The professors of the fetish were the exponents of voodoo, a form of devil-worship originating in West Africa and taken over to the States of America at the time of slave trafficking, and it is in this form of black magic that the fetish has its cradle and is exploited professionally, with sacrifice (at one time human) and elaborate ceremony.

Of course, in the sophisticated society in which we now live such practices are dismissed as naïvely primitive; notwithstanding, the relics of such beliefs still linger on, so that we make a fetish of throwing salt over our left shoulder, or assiduously avoid walking under ladders. In the same way, modern man acknowledges a light-hearted though quite emphatic comfort in the carrying or wearing of similar charms of protection as did his ancestors. Thus even today people consider stones with a natural perforation through them to be lucky. In olden times a necklace was made of these lucky stones and hung up behind the door of a house in order to preserve the inhabitants from the evil influence of witches and the evil eye. Throughout the ages it has been generally believed that stones were powerful charms against misfortune. There is a claim made that the millionaire J. D. Rockefeller was never without his lucky eagle stone, which talisman, kept on his person, offered him constant assurance of wealth and well-being. For those whose tastes might be deemed more aesthetic (or commercial), precious stones possessed magical properties also. The diamond was worn as a talisman in battle and was also highly valued as a healer for fever. Similarly, the turquoise was associated with health, the notion prevailing that, as the health of the wearer of a turquoise varied, so the hue of the stone oscillated. Another powerful talisman was the amethyst; giving protection against theft, it also made its wearer irresistible to the fair sex. The sapphire on the other hand was believed to encourage chastity, for which reason tradition claimed that Pope Innocent III (1198–1217) commanded all bishops to wear sapphire rings. It goes without saying that to find a prelate wearing such episcopal insignia and to enquire whether the sapphire was in fact efficacious would not only be counted impertinent, but would also probably be fruitless, for as with so many superstitions which have remained to the present day, their significance and origin have been lost in time. Yet there remains that trait in man which clings to traditional notions and relics with irrational determination, regardless of reason or knowledge. It was this characteristic which presumably accounted for the otherwise unfathomable practice of using stone tools in ceremonial functions long after the Stone Age had been superseded by that of iron. Why else should flint knives have been preserved in the rite of circumcision by Jews, or been used by the priests of Baal at occasions of high festival when they gashed themselves in order to obtain the favour of their god? Equally one might well ask why the Egyptian process of embalming required a first incision of the body with a knife of Ethopian stone. Or indeed why Hannibal insisted upon a flint knife for the sacrificial lamb which was offered up before he went into battle against Scipio. The only explanation would appear to be that such ritual had always been performed with implements of stone, and in order to maintain the beneficial results, such ritual must contrive to employ the identical tools. So conservative religious taboo decreed.

WITH THIS RING

While there is no evidence of rings set with precious stones being incorporated into religious ceremony (the wearing of such an ornament being specifically the decision of the individual), the plain circlet of precious metal is almost the integral symbol of the marriage service. Worthy explanations are offered as to its significance and origin, but sustained investigation has proved that all evidence is speculative. The truth concerning wedding rings appears to be that the precise reason for their existence is unknown. It can be said that wedding rings have been unearthed from Egyptian tombs, that Juvenal wrote in his Satire VI that the Romans used them. Swinburne, in his *Treatise of Spousals*, waxes plausible when he writes that, 'the ring being circular, that is round and without end,' is a symbol for the married couple 'that their mutual love and hearty affection shall roundly flow from one to the other as in a circle, and that continually and for ever.'

Does this explanation match the implication that a wedding ring is simply a symbol of state? Or does it rather suggest that its use was, like that of other amulets, protective—a sacred protective circlet of love and marriage? Only speculation is possible since here, as with the flint-stone knife, certain answers are lost in time. It might be added, however, that American negroes greatly favour rings (made of horseshoe nails) as charms of protection.

LOVE CHARMS

If a ring grew to be associated with true love, there must be countless charms for initiating love or rekindling it. One such was the mandrake. Hedged about with numerous taboos and possessed of mysterious properties and powers, this plant, whose root subdivided so that the main trunk with its appendages brought to mind the form and limbs of a human being, was believed to utter terrifying shrieks when uprooted, and after certain treatment could be made into a gallowsman. In Germany in fact, the mandrake is called the *Galgenmann-chen*, or 'little Gallowsman', and regarded as the devil's own plant. It was consequently believed therefore that anyone who possessed a gallowsman must have sold himself to the devil.

In early Canaanite tradition, the mandrake was associated with fertility: Genesis 30.14 describes how Reuben, son of Jacob's first wife Leah, found some of these plants growing in a field and took them home to his mother. There followed some hard bargaining by Rachel, the favourite but barren wife of Jacob who coveted their possession. The story has an ironic twist at the end, however, for in spite of procuring the prized mandrake to cure her childlessness, it was nevertheless Leah and not Rachel who conceived.

An interesting record concerning love potions is found in Masse's works. He declared, 'I have seen men so deeply enamoured of women as to fall sick and wander distracted through the fields. They thought it came of a potion of wine, mixed with cantharides, and other things which I shall not specify, lest the evil disposed may take advantage of it.' The efficiency of amatory potions or philtres, unquestioned in an earlier age, but then falling into disrepute, is however, returning to favour.

In the United States of America the seventies have seen the revival of the dragon's blood love potion, and it seems that, whereas in the last century it was the resort of love-lorn girls in the less salubrious districts of London, it is now enjoying a renewed and highly fashionable popularity amongst the emancipated and progressive young women in the New World. The notion holds that a packet of dragon's blood (which transpires to be the gum used in wood-staining), if burned at midnight on a Friday, will, without fail, rekindle the affections of a lover whose ardour has cooled.

Another love charm whose roots are buried in antiquity yet which still flourishes is the string of love beads. The author was told recently that the Indians of the Navajo tribe are doing a brisk trade selling these charms in American cities. Nylon-threaded berries, they purport to be unique Indian beads containing ancient ingredients for enchanting a desired lover, and advanced and educated though the market is, trade for such love philtres is satisfactorily brisk.

DEFENSIVE DEVICES

An amulet whose origins are more easily explained is the resplendent breastplate of the Life Guards. Now a decorative part of their insignia, it yet remains a quaint survival of the time when breastplates and shields were a practical method of protection. This is not, however, to deny that even when such impediments were in ordinary use their users did not endow them with added, magical, powers of defence. The Shoshonees of North America were known to believe that their shields possessed a supernatural power which made them impenetrable, and it was the fanatical belief in their enchantment that made the uprising of Jamaican slaves in 1760 so reckless in their enterprise.

The sign of the cross is an understandable token of protection and where it is made knowingly is a prayer or testimony. There are found, however, countless instances where its sign is taken in vain and used superstitiously. Part of the mandrake-up-rooting ritual required the making of the sign of the cross over the plant three times lest the agent digging it up should be struck by the mandrake's supernatural powers and die. In the same way, though no builder would ever acknowledge or even realise it, windows of newly built structures are daubed with whitewash crosses. Innocent common sense explains the ritual as the natural precaution taken to show that the window frames have been glazed and must not any longer be taken as open apertures for ladder thrusts. To the man familiar with supernatural tradition, however, the white crosses are an undeniable claim for protection against evil spirits entering the empty building.

Ineradicably established in superstition is the power of trees. Because of their growth and movement they were seen to possess vitality, and to the artless mind of primitive man this mysterious movement and change indicated an invisible and therefore supernatural power. Thus trees feature widely in superstitious tradition; and even as symbols of good or ill fortune traditions are diverse. In the heyday of the Red Indian the Iroquois tribe fashioned miniature canoes as talismans to protect them from drowning, while the Hopi Indians immunised themselves from infection by wearing amulets of wood.

Then, quite apart from wooden idols which prevailed universally as household gods for the succour of their possessors, there are found instances of other employment of trees as divine protectors. In Japan it was sufficient to chant 'Kuwabara!' (mulberry plantation) if caught out of doors during a storm. This insured against a lightning strike since the thunder-god would never attack a mulberry grove and, hearing its name called out, he could be deceived. Lesser spirits might, in the Middle East, be diverted from malevolent courses by fanning the woodsmoke of cedar in their direction, and in Arabia there prevailed a notion that any household having some Egyptian thorn within it could rest content from fear of intrusion by evil spirits, since the thorn was 'Mother of Satyrs', the woodland sprites whose care was the preservation of tranquillity in the home. Yet another tree, the coconut, was a potent force because of the eyes in its fruit. Being able to see, as was thought, it could thus control the direction or timing of its fall and had the power of avoiding collision with objects in its path. Presumably such powers would also enable it to meet its target more easily should its inclination prefer the alternative course.

Trees also have a say in good or bad luck in Britain, though their power is propitiated rather differently. While the simple possession of a rowan (or mountain ash) in one's garden was believed to keep witches at bay, it was the cut stem of hawthorn—and essentially broken off on Ascension Day—which offered protection against lightning. Contrary to the superstition surrounding the cedar woodsmoke, to burn a holly tree, even now, is to cry out for immediate misfortune. (The lively belief in this particular superstition can be vouched for by the author who met vigorous opinion for it in some rural parts of Wales).

DUMB INFLUENCE

Another superstition still practised today in country districts is spitting for luck when you see a white horse. There is some variance in the reasons given for doing so, some spitting to protect themselves from unforeseen calamity, and some simply to claim good fortune, but about the beast and its colour opinion is unanimous. It might well reflect back to the tradition that the god Woden was claimed always to travel on horseback and without fail on an albino. Horses, however, take a place in superstitious tradition in their own right, particularly in Germany where it is said that early tribes used to hang up the actual heads of horses killed in battle as an offering to the deities. For the same reason a whole beast would be sacrificed to them, such a beast being the only kind deemed worthy. Conversely, because of the high esteem in which it was held, the horse had to be protected, and it was from this necessity that horse-brasses developed. Amongst the earliest of amulets, brasses—or crescents as they were also known—were claimed to be in use in Europe and the Near East in Roman times. Biblical evidence confirms their establishment in Canaan even as far back as the late Bronze Age for Judges 8.21,26 describes how Gideon, Judge in Israel, took the crescents that were about the necks of the camels of Zebah and Zalmunna, kings of Midian, as trophies of war. These crescents, which later became known almost exclusively as horse-brasses, could be made in many designs, the traditional ones being of a crescent moon, or related to the sun and thus in the shapes of a rayed disk, the wheel, or the swastika. Their purpose, however, was single: they were believed to protect their wearer from the power of witchcraft and the evil eye.

The cat is classically associated as a sacred animal with Egypt in the time of the Pharaohs. Together with the fox and hare, it was also incorporated into the rites of primitive religion in ancient Britain. All three were totemic beasts and their devotees believed that, if they carried some part of one about their person, they would be protected by the animal they worshipped. It is doubtful whether rabbits existed in Britain

until the coming of the Normans in 1066, but it is certain that
before the arrival of Christianity the hare was used in pagan
religious practices. It was the superstition attaching to the hare
which was later transferred to the rabbit, which creature itself
seems to have inherited the magical properties. So in mediaeval
England the popular belief was established that on Easter Eve
rabbits acquired the ability to lay eggs, and in rural areas
people used to say that, if you caught a rabbit in the churchyard and cut off its left foreleg, then good luck would attend
you as long as you had it in possession. It is obviously this
tradition from which the rabbits' foot charm derives; and being
bound up in Easter beliefs revolving around rabbits and eggs,
it is easy to see how it came to be loved by children.

There is at the present time a wave of belief in the power of
the owl to bring success in academic study, and in America's
university centres owl charms are enjoying a landslide popularity. Being from ancient Greek times the symbol of wisdom,
it is not difficult to see how this fetish has developed. The owl
is not the only bird associated with luck; nor is the notorious
albatross whose death at sea brings down such dire disaster
upon those mariners who cause it. Just as common in superstitious tradition are the swallow, the magpie and the robin.
The nest of the swallow is considered lucky, and the bird itself
is protected by imaginary penalties. This ancient belief is as
common in England as it is in Germany, and even in China the
swallow's nest is considered lucky and its life inviolate; though
at one time it was fear that saved the swallow from injury in
Ireland, since it was believed that every swallow had in him
three drops of the devil's blood. The robin was considered a
'blessed bird' from its association with the crucifixion, and it
was said that if you should take the eggs from a robin's nest
you would get your legs broken; while if you had the misfortune to have a robin die in your hand, that member would
be affected with a continuous shaking.

Just as calamitous was the accident of seeing a magpie. A
pair was of no consequence, but a single bird heralded horrible
consequences. Because the likelihood of coming across just one
was so common, however, a remedy was vital to nullify its
malific power, and this was the formula that would save the
situation: having made the sign of the cross with the toe

of a shoe and then spitting, the following jingle was recited:

'I cross one magpie,
An' one magpie cross me;
May the devil take th' magpie
An' God take me.'

Making the sign of the cross in a circle on the ground and reciting the first two lines of Psalm 68 was the antidote for unwittingly calling down misfortune upon oneself through the accidental sight of a snake. This was said to be the reason why St Patrick chose a shamrock as Ireland's national flower: in part, and on religious grounds, because the shamrock, having three leaves, represented the Trinity, but largely, and on extremely basic grounds, because 'no serpent will touch a shamrock'.

Intriguing for its roots of derivation is the John Dory fish, venerated by the Greeks who associated it with their supreme god, Zeus. A lucky fish, it was believed to have earned its name thus: 'Dory' was said to be derived from the French *adorée*, worshipped, and 'John' was taken as a corruption of *jaune*, yellow, from the golden hue the fish turns when taken from the water. According to some authorities the dark spot on this fish was made by the thumb and finger of St Peter when he picked it up at his Lord's command to obtain the tribute money; which suggestion has in turn led some authorities to claim that the name Dory is derived from *il janitore*, 'doorkeeper', referring to St Peter's office of retaining the keys of heaven.

'O superstitious dainty, Peter's fish;
How cam'st thou here to make so goodly dish?'
(*Dialogues of Metellus.* 1693)

SALT FOR SORROW

Perhaps two of the most common and widely accepted superstitions with a bearing on luck are the horseshoe for good luck, and spilling of salt for bad, both of which are acknowledged virtually the world over. The only remedy for spilling salt is to take a pinch of what was upset with the right-hand thumb and finger and to cast it over the left shoulder.

Because it was thought that the devil slyly insinuated himself in the scattered grains, the action of throwing them over the left shoulder was necessary to atone for the carelessness of allowing such a precious substance to fall to the ground. Salt has ever been regarded not only as the symbol of incorruption and immortality (and therefore hated by the devil and the powers of darkness) but also as a symbol of friendship. Thus spilt salt was a sign of breaking friendship—a notion dramatically illustrated in Leonardo da Vinci's famous picture *The Last Supper*, where the artist depicted Judas Iscariot standing beside the overturned salt-cellar.

The ancient Jews used salt in their sacrifices, as did the Greeks and Romans; and it has been recorded that the Arabs of Egypt threw it into the fire for protection against the curse of the evil eye. So salt has become established from time immemorial as a protective, purifying and precious substance.

A final superstition connected with salt is summed up in the proverb: 'Give neither counsel nor salt unless asked for it', and even to this day the phrase 'helping people to salt' is interpreted by some as helping people to sorrow. This is perhaps the reason why, when superstitious people are asked for the salt at table, they pass it towards the person who requires it but will never put it into his hand or expect thanks for it.

HORSEHOE POWER

The horseshoe has much happier potential. Probably the most common good-luck symbol in use today, even though it no longer graces so many thresholds as it was said to do by Aubrey in the seventeenth century, nevertheless the horseshoe still spreads its influence of good fortune over a wide range, appearing in replica form on wedding cakes, car key-rings, greetings, get-well cards, and the like. The origin of this superstition lies in the fact that horseshoes were made of iron, which was noted for its ancient power of giving protection from witches, fairies and devils. To give themselves immunity from the plague, the Romans used to knock iron nails into the walls of their dwellings, and the saying, 'touch iron' was as common in early days in Britain as 'touch wood' is at present. Magical properties were attached to iron as soon as the metal was discovered and used for weaponry. The tribe with the superior weapons were considered to be wielding a magical influence over those possessing only stone or wooden weapons, and even when iron became common the 'magic' built up around the use of the metal became associated with the metal itself. To find a horseshoe used to be considered the height of good fortune, but to keep that good fortune the finder had to ensure that the traditional ritual was observed. The horseshoe had to be picked up with the right hand, and after spitting on one of the horns of the shoe and making a wish, the finder had to throw it backwards over his left shoulder and go on his way without turning to see where it had landed.

THE WAY OF LADY LUCK

Perhaps in no country is superstitious ritual more elaborate and vital than in India. The Hindus seem to have gathered together the superstitions of the ages, and to have kept on adding to them until they have arrived at a code that can seldom be matched anywhere in the world. Among those who still practise these superstitions, none are more exacting, or rigorously adhered to, than those connected with the building of a new house. First it is necessary to wait for the lucky hour of the lucky day, and when both coincide, the prospective builder may venture abroad to choose an appropriate site for his house. To meet en route, however, a snake, a man with either a broad or bald head, a Brahmin, a sick or blind person, a person without a nose, an oil merchant, barber, or a woman who has no breasts —any one of these encounters augures disaster for the proposed enterprise, and the planner would be far better advised to wait for another day. On the other hand, should he meet a young virgin on that journey, then he could be sure that the gods indeed smiled on him and all would be well.

In our materialistic, practical way of living in the West, we would regard it at least as eccentric (if not plain laughable) to allow such trivialities to distract our purposes. At the same time, to come across a cantankerous colleague at the beginning of the day can well draw from us the comment, 'I say, Tom, Dick, or Harry, has got out of bed on the wrong foot this morning', quite unaware that such an exclamation is nothing less than acknowledgement of the ancient supposition that it was unlucky to start the day with one's left foot first.

The preacher in the Book of Ecclesiastes expressed the same sentiment poetically if inaccurately when he wrote, 'a wise man's heart is at his right hand, but a fool's heart at his left'—a notion echoed by Pythagoras when he taught that it was essential to put a shoe on the right foot first, also that it was unlucky to enter a house or leave a room with the left foot foremost. These seemingly childish suppositions stem from the primitive belief that giving preference to the right side of the body was considered the demonstration of man's prime duty of deference to the gods.

It is probably true to say that the majority of continued superstitions hark back to an original blueprint, as is true of the competitors in the Folk Sports Olympiad on the island of Gotland who blow on a stone for luck because hundreds of years ago, at the end of the eighth century, their ancestors, the Vikings, on their way to raid Britain observed the tradition of wearing hammer-shaped stone amulets to bring them victory. Some superstitious observances, on the other hand, are purely individual and proved by chance. Thus it is said that Jack Nicklaus, the great American golfer, confessed that when his game was going well he was meticulously careful to follow the good fortune pattern where preparations, breakfast menu, and travelling route to the golf course were concerned, lest deviation in one iota should interfere with the excellence of his strokes. On a much more obscure level it may be admitted that the author's wife sometimes feels it of paramount importance to walk in the squares of pavement blocks, telling herself that to step on a line will mean some tiresome misfortune like the further delay of the letter she has long awaited, the sickening of one of the children, or the failure of her husband's latest book!

Thus there grew up, alongside the lucky charms, the other superstitious foibles of people—a favourite dress or tie; a lucky pattern of events; the ominous signs in the haphazard events of the day. And although modern man may have moved away from wearing amulets in the shape of the crescent moon as a charm to aid conception and to bring increase of crops and herds, even though we may have outgrown the influence of deep superstitions, yet it can be said that a great majority of people still must, if frank, admit to some susceptibility to the power of the fates, even though it may only be a frivolous acknowledgement that they touch wood, carry lucky charms or use favourite numbers when choosing lottery tickets or filling in football coupons. Perhaps it is significant that among the ancients the goddess of Fortune was represented as a blindfolded dispenser of good luck or bad, who had cornucopia, and often a wheel in her hands as an emblem of inconstancy.

CHAPTER SEVEN

Outside Influences

GENERALLY SPEAKING, the derivatives of many superstitious beliefs have become light-hearted. Those relating back
to cosmic signs, however, tend to bear a more weighty influence
upon mankind, tinged with the same awesome fear as attends
superstitions akin to witchcraft. The very mystery of the
heavenly bodies with their physical power over the behaviour
of the earth compel man's respectful attention. Having ascribed
them divine power, he has, down the ages, watched them,
attempted to interpret their signs and in consequence learned
to predict his future from them. The jocular lip-service paid
to the magazine's horoscope page, more often than would be
admitted, bears an underlying reluctant credence, while the
power of the moon upon our lives might in some cases be described as medical. Bound up with the science of the stars is
their lesser study, astrology. This sprang into influential
existence almost with time itself, and derived from it is the
relevance of number mystique and dreams.

MOONSHINE

In our generation—until the astronauts landed on it at any
rate, and thereby dispelled some of the enchantment—our
notion of the moon has been of a romantic orb, in a night of
soft music and love's first kiss. Matched against the moon's
superstitious relevance, this notion might have some aesthetic
value, for in far-distant times the moon was regarded as
influencing fertility, and later as a deity peculiarly related to
woman. It was thus thought to be the source and origin of the
female ability to bear children and was looked upon as the
goddess who kept watch over all matters of special concern
since remote times. These notions existed among the primitive
tribes of Polynesia, Australia, Greenland, among the black
peoples of Africa, and the Indians of both South and North

America. The people of ancient Greece and Rome, China, India, Syria and Arabia, and the Celtic peoples of Western and Northern Europe incorporated these beliefs about the moon into the heart of their religious structures. We ourselves are not considered impervious to the moon's power, for it is still felt to be lucky to see a new moon as long as it is not through glass. And perhaps we still observe the age-old ritual of looking at the moon over our left shoulder, curtsy or bow, or take out money and turn it over, so that the moon, 'the Increaser', may multiply it for us. The respect denoted in the bow or curtsy showed clearly the high regard in which the moon was held. Thus it is in keeping that some of the older generation even of our day can remember being told as children that it was wicked and disrespectful to try to count the stars or point a finger at the moon. These are simple superstitious rituals and perhaps ridiculous to a generation of canny realists, but they are fundamental, for they can all be found in the ancient worship of the Greek moon goddess, Hecate, where they are parts of elaborate ceremonials.

Part of the Greeks' adoration consisted in offering to the moon (as well as to Apollo and Diana) cakes with 'horns'. Circular and marked with a cross, these cakes represented the moon and her four quarters.

Isis was the principal goddess of the ancient Egyptians and was identified with the moon; and the cow was regarded as sacred to her, its horns symbolising the crescent of the moon which, from Egypt, is seen lying on its back. (Though perhaps far fetched, the mind is nonetheless tickled by the possible comparison with this idea of the nursery rhyme, 'Hey diddle diddle, the cat and the fiddle, the cow jumped over the moon.') The Hindus consider the hare to be sacred to the moon on the other hand, because the outline shape of a hare can be seen in the full moon.

Fraught with ominous meaning was the waning or dying moon. To cut your hair at such a time when in England, France or Iceland, was to staunch its growth for the rest of your days. Then with sensible logic, it was thought a sickness would more readily yield to medication and fade if its treatment coincided with the waning moon. Contrariwise, the crops would be more successful if the seed had been sown when the moon was young.

In parts of Germany, a morbid offshoot of this notion flourished in the belief that if the father of a family had to die, then it were better that he did so when the moon was waxing, for if he went when the moon was old, there was a danger that he would gradually take the whole family with him and the line would die out.

Being so influential, the moon required the protective eye of her subjects. Thus the ancient Greeks, believing that an eclipse of the heavenly bodies meant their ravage by demons, sought to ward off the attack by crying out 'I see you'. Similarly, elsewhere among primitive peoples, a fearful cacophony of drums, shouting and hullabaloo was set up at an eclipse to 'frighten away the terrible monster that was bent on devouring the sun and the moon'. Still other interpretations were offered of this phenomenon, like that of the ancient Mexicans, who thought an eclipse was the result of a quarrel between the sun and moon, in which one or other emerged from the tussle black and blue. The ancient tribes in North America went further: whenever a visible eclipse of the sun took place, the Indians were thrown into the greatest distress, for they believed the sun to be dying. But there was still a chance to resuscitate him, they believed, and in order to bring him to life again they would stick burning coals on the points of their arrows and shoot them upwards to rekindle the object of their adoration.

COSMIC CONCERN

Signs in the sky have ever been regarded as religious omens. The rainbow, for example, was regarded as the symbol of God's promise never again to destroy the world with a flood, whereas our Norse forebears regarded the rainbow as a bridge between this world and the next. In England the Milky Way was at one time believed to be the path to heaven, and Roman Catholic children believed that a shooting star was in fact a soul released from purgatory. Signs by which the gods communicated to men a knowledge of future events were termed omens, auguries and prodigies. The latter were regarded as direct manifestations of the wrath of heaven: so thunder and lightning, earthquakes, an eclipse of the moon or sun were considered unlucky signs in the heavens. It was believed, nonetheless, that this wrath might be appeased should the right prayers and sacrifices be offered to the offended powers. One especially efficacious means of appeasement was the ringing of a church bell and in the churchwardens' accounts Spalding parish, there reads an entry: '1519 it'm pd. for ryngng when the Temest was, iijd'.

So dependent upon the supposed deliverance by bells did people become that explicit provision for this purpose was made in the consecration of church bells. It was elaborate. The service began with a litany and a series of antiphonal psalms. The bell to be blessed was washed with holy water which contained salt; afterwards it was wiped and then anointed with holy oil, four times on the inside and seven times on the outside. An old Paris ritual included these words in the blessing of church bells: 'May the sound of this bell put to flight the fiery darts of the enemy of man, the ravages of thunder and lightning, the rapid fall of stones, the disasters of tempests, . . .' With so much attention and ritual focused on the consecration of bells and such admission of their protective properties, it was no wonder that people set such store by them. Useless were these words of Naorgeorgus:

'The shaven priests before them marche, ye people follow
    fast,
Still striving who shall gather first ye bowes yt downe are
    cast,
For falsely they believe yt these have force and virtue greate,
Against ye rage of winter stormes and thunder's flashing
    heate.'

(*Naorgeorgus*, translated by Barnaby Googe)

The people had grasped steadfastly the notion that church bells would save them not only from cosmic wrath but from evil spirits likewise, should they have the good fortune to live within the hearing of the bell. Thus it was no wonder that this jingle became so popularly known:

'Men's death I tell	By doleful knell;
Lightning and thunder	I break asunder;
On Sabbath all	To church I call,
The sleepy head	I raise from bed;
The winds so fierce	I do disperse
Men's cruel rage	I do assuage.'

Bells ward off evil in other continents than Europe: in central Africa, no sooner is a Muganda child out of its cradle than its parents give it an anklet or bracelet of bells to protect it from the molesting attention of evil spirits.

There were from time to time, however, malevolent portents in the heavens which augured catastrophe for whole communities or even nations and against which there was no redress at all. In 1603 a calamity reminiscent of the visions in the Book of Revelation befell Cracow in Poland. Simon Goulart wrote of it: 'On the 29th of March, 1545, about eight o'clock in the morning, there fell in the neighbourhood of Cracow, a thunder-bolt, with a clap of thunder so violent as seemed to shake all Poland. Immediately there appeared in the heavens three red crosses, between which was a man completely armed, holding a flaming sword, and combating an army, which he defeated. Thereupon followed a horrible Dragon, which swallowed up the victorious combatant; and upon this the heavens opened, as if on fire, and was thus beheld for the space of a full hour. Next there appeared three Rainbows, with their accustomed colours, on the highest of which was the figure of an *Angel*, as usually represented, in the shape of a youth with wings at the shoulders; holding the Sun in one hand the moon in the other. This second spectacle having continued half an hour, in the presence of all who chose to look at it, some clouds then arose, which covered these apparitions.'

BLAZING STARS

Such cosmic heraldry would make the most cynical of men pause to consider. No wonder then that ignorant and superstitious people were baffled. And thus perplexed, it was natural that they should seek some explanation for these signs and have studied the consequences that followed them. The comets as portents of disaster seem to have been one of the most ancient and widely accepted popular superstitions. According to Suetonius a blazing star was seen by the Romans soon after the assassination of Julius Caesar.

'A little ere the mighty Julius fell,
The graves stood tenantless, and the sheeted dead
Did squeak and gibber in the Roman streets:

As stars with trains of fire and dews of blood,
Disasters in the sun.'
                                        (Shakespeare: *Hamlet I. i*)

Another comet of import was that which appeared in 1060. With the Norman Conquest six years later in that best-known of years, 1066, it was no wonder the people of Britain marked the astral body as significant.

The appearance of Halley's comet in 1456, just as the Turks had become masters of Constantinople and threatened to move into Europe, was regarded by Christendom with superstitious dread, and to the Ave Maria was added the prayer: 'Lord save us from the devil, the Turk, and the comet.'

A blazing star, or comet, appeared for several months before the London Plague of 1665, as did another the year after, a little before the Great Fire. 'I saw both these Stars,' writes Daniel De Foe, 'and I must confess, had so much of the common notion of such things in my head, that I was apt to look upon them as the forerunners and warnings of God's judgements; and especially when, after the Plague had followed the first, I yet saw another of the like kind, I could not but say, "God has not yet sufficiently scourged the City".'

Lilly, in his *Astrological Predictions* published in 1648, predicted this catastrophe. He maintained that it would be 'ominous to London, unto her Merchants at Sea, to her traffique at land, to her poor, to her rich, to all sorts of people inhabiting in her or her Liberties, by reason of sundry Fires and a consuming Plague.'

ASTROLOGY

This development of studying the cosmic signs was perhaps a natural consequence. Faced with such mysteries, man would attempt to appease the powers concerned; and he would also try to understand them, and perhaps, by that, find a way at least to predict the precise nature of what they heralded even if he could not by that understanding avert the evil he foresaw! This was the origin of Astrology, the supposed method of discovering future events by means of the various positions of the heavenly bodies. Astrology was universally practised among the nations of antiquity, excepting the Greeks. Among the

Romans it was practised from the time of the conquest of Egypt, and all the followers of Mohammed have ever been firm believers in it.

Very early in the history of mankind a belief arose that there was a close connection between the fate of man and the positions and movements of the heavenly bodies. It was thought that the position of the heavenly bodies at the moment of a person's birth would directly affect that person's life, and that any undertaking which might be considered must not be pursued until the positions of the heavenly bodies had been determined to see whether or not the undertaking would be successful.

Probably the oldest pseudo-science in the world, astrology was one of the first attempts to explain the riddle of existence in a mathematical and scientific shape. It is based on observance and experiment; the time of birth recorded and the state of the heavens noted; any serious illness or domestic tragedy was observed and compared with the signs in the heavens. These results were then compared with findings of other astrologers, leading to a huge accumulation of literature about the occult heavens. While the bulk of learned mankind has never looked on the casting of horoscopes as more than an amusement, the credulous have exalted it to the position of a powerful religious cult.

The astrologer, while doing little to come to terms with scientific knowledge of the universe, has successfully adapted himself to changing conditions. Werenefels recorded that a superstitious man 'will be more afraid of the Constellation-fires than the flame of his next-door neighbour's house. He will not open a vein till he has asked leave of the planets. He will avoid the sea whenever Mars is in the middle of Heaven lest that warrior god should stir up pirates against him. In Taurus he will plant his trees, that this sign, which the astrologers are pleased to call fix'd, may fasten them deeper in the earth. He will make use of no herbs but such as are gathered in the planetary hour. Against any sort of misfortune he will arm himself with a ring, to which he has fixed the benevolent aspect of the stars' (*Dissertation upon Superstition*).

In *The Man of Law's Tale* Chaucer illustrates the obsession of people of the Middle Ages with astrology.

'And Mars will slay this marriage, if she marry.
O thou unfortunate oblique degree
Of the Ecliptic, when the cadent Mars,
Thrust from his proper angle, helplessly
Falls into Scorpio, darkest house of stars!'

Chaucer thus suggests that the contrary motions of the planets are the reason for the failure of Canstance's marriage 'because of the evil influence of Mars in Scorpio, which is the house of death, battle, travail and harm.'

The *Sunday Times* in Britain estimated recently that over two-thirds of the adults in Britain read their horoscopes, and of these approximately a fifth, some seven million, take them seriously. Asia is teeming with millions of superstitious star-gazers; almost every Hindu marriage in India is based on a horoscope. France, Germany, and America are becoming centres of the ancient cult of astrology. For the price of a daily newspaper or journal you can discover, if you were born between 24 July and 23 August, under the zodiac sign of Leo, that 'you are generous, magnetic, dynamic, vital,' and that 'you possess an unforgettable personality'. For a little more hard cash you can purchase a ready-made oriental horoscope which carries the information that the oriental zodiac, like that in the West, has twelve divisions, but each lasts a year instead of a month. Depicted by an animal symbol, each year—together with the people born in it—is endowed with special qualities. The Rat, Buffalo, Tiger, Cat, Dragon, Snake, Horse, Goat, Monkey, Cockerel, Dog and Boar are the symbols, and each one is either Yin or Yang, the female and male principles. Such an oriental horoscope invites you to 'Look up your birth date in the chart, then read on to find out what the Chinese think about you.' Not only will you find that 'Michael Wilding is a Rat', but also that the Boars like Cromwell, Chiang Kai-Shek, Field-Marshal Montgomery, and Terence Rattigan 'are often flirtatious. Some of them are obsessed with sex. They are more Yin than Yang.'

There are those, however, who run their lives by the zodiac and will pay enormous sums for consultations with their favourite astrologers. Adolf Hitler employed as many as five astrologers to advise and counsel him on his star-gazing path to 'victory'. Writing of the situation in America, Eric Marple in his *Superstition and the Superstitious* (1971) claimed that 'the computer horoscope industry has more recently become a multi-million dollar enterprise in the United States and according to a Press report one such concern anticipates an annual sale of half a million horoscopes in respect of children, personnel directors and business corporations'. Astral advice on mergers and takeovers is a speciality in this field. In the words of one brochure: 'Company astrology is destined to branch out into the open.'

LUCKY 7

Astrologers once maintained that the planet Saturn presided over the seventh and ninth years and their odd multiples in a person's life, which were then referred to as the *climacteric years*. These years were thought to bring great changes and dangers in the life-span, the most dangerous of all being when a person attained the age of sixty-three—an age few people at that time were thought able to reach.

'There be', said Fabian Withers, 'certain evil times and years of a man's life which are at every seven years' end. Wherefore if thou wilt prolong thy days, as often as thou comest to every seventh or ninth year (if thou givest any credit to Marsilius Ficinus), diligently consult with an astronomer, from whence and by what means any peril or danger may happen, or come unto thee; then either go unto a physician, or use discretion and temperance, and by that means thou mayest defer and prolong thy natural life, through the rules of astronomy and the help of the physician.' Even to this day there are people who believe that a person changes completely every seven years. In Carmarthenshire, a farmer recently said that his son—who had suffered from asthma since he was a baby and had now reached the age of eighteen—would probably be cured when he was twenty-one. His doctors, he said, maintained that the child's seventh birthday would bring a change, or if not then, seven years later when the boy was fourteen. Even with two disappointments behind him, the hope was still bright, and the accomplishment of the next seven years was apprehended with vital hope.

In Eyam churchyard, Derbyshire, a tombstone carried an

epitaph recording this superstition relative to the time of death.

> 'Here lieth the body of Ann Sellars, buried by this
> stone, who dyed on January 15, 1731.
> Likewise here lise dear Isaac Sellars, my husband and my
> right,
> Who was buried on the same day come seven years, 1738.
> In seven years time there comes a change—
> Observe and here you'll see
> On that same day come seven years
> My husband laid by me.'

The number seven has an attraction about it. It is magnetic, it is satisfying. The Bible makes ample use of this number from Genesis to Revelation. The creation of the world was completed by the seventh day, just as it was on the seventh day that Jericho fell to Israel. Jacob served seven years for Rachel, and the ears of corn and the cows of Pharaoh's dream came in sevens. As the ritual mechanics of the Torah worked often in sevens, so the visions of St John the Divine revelled in the perfect number. Balaam bade Balach build 'seven altars and prepare seven oxen and seven rams'; Elijah on Mount Carmel sent his servant to look for signs of rain seven times; while his successor Elisha, sent Naaman the Syrian leper to wash in the Jordan seven times, and brought the widow's son fully back to life after seven sneezes.

In the Gospels Mary Magdalene was cleansed of seven devils, Simon Peter was told that seven acts of forgiveness could never suffice, and seven loaves of bread wonderfully fed four thousand people. There is, in fact, almost universal acclaim for the number seven. And also favoured by the ancients were the numbers forty and three.

THREE

Pythagoras maintained that three was a perfect number, and life supports this in its manifestation that the world is after all made up of three elements, air, sea, and earth, while man likewise comprises three dimensions: body, mind and spirit. Faith, hope and charity are the three main Christian graces, while the world, the flesh, and the devil are man's perpetual enemies. The concept of the Trinity as well, and this is a concept not peculiar to Christianity, was made up of three: Father, Son and Holy Spirit.

Fairy tales, while acknowledging seven dwarfs and forty thieves, also make great use of the number three; three bears, three little pigs, three princesses, and three blind mice. Then there are three wishes granted, three chances given, and three tasks to be accomplished. The heathen of ancient Greece and Rome also regarded the number three as being mystical, for we learn there were three Graces, three Fates, and three Furies.

To the Jews as well, three was looked upon as a magic number, so that we read of three men coming to Abraham to predict the birth of his son Isaac. Similarly it was with three darts that Joab pierced Absolom through the heart; Jonah was in the belly of the whale for three days and nights; and Balaam's ass is said to have asked, 'What have I done to you that you strike me three times?'

UNLUCKY FOR SOME

Odd numbers were regarded as being holy, for Pythagoras recommended that oblations to the celestial be made in unequal numbers. Those to the infernal deity, however, were in numbers that were equal. Causes for celebration among European nations are marked by the firing of an odd number of guns, and there was a time when events judged to be disastrous for the nation were recorded by an even number.

From time immemorial thirteen has been regarded as an unlucky number, but the fact that thirteen sat at the Last Supper before Christ was crucified heightened the significance of this superstition in countries which became influenced by Christianity. It is found, however, in Norse mythology too. The story of Baldur, who attended a banquet in Valhalla, tells how he was murdered after the god Loki gatecrashed the feast making the thirteenth guest.

Even in the bureaucratic halls of the twentieth century, thirteen is deferred to as a number with power for misfortune, since we find both in Italy as well as in Britain, a frequent omission of number thirteen by Councils when they number the houses in streets. Registration numbers for cars also, and lotteries, sometimes jump from twelve to fourteen.

A brave stand against this way of thinking was made by Woodrow Wilson, the American president. He maintained that, far from being unlucky, thirteen was in fact quite the opposite. Apart from the fact that thirteen had turned up in connection with every outstanding success he had ever had in his career, were there not, he reminded people, thirteen stars in the first American flag, and thirteen colonies that made up the Republic? So common was the 'unlucky thirteen' superstition in America at the beginning of the twentieth century that it was deliberately flouted by 'Thirteen Clubs' and 'Thirteen Diners'. A London newspaper of that time carried the following report:

New York Jan. 16.

'Superstition was flouted and invited to do its worst by all manners of taunts levelled against the fearsome number thirteen at a banquet given in New York last night by the members of the Thirteen Club.

The club contains many more than thirteen members, but the diners sat at tables thirteen to each. Before each plate a red candle burned in a death's head holder, and the member whose candle went out first was supposed to receive it as a sign. As soon as the company was seated a new mirror was broken.

The ices were served in the form of a skull reposing in a coffin. The toastmaster used a forearm bone to rap for order. At intervals the diners counted up to thirteen as a chant, the number thirteen being hailed with cheers. At the close of the banquet the waiters filed into the room to the music of the funeral march, each waiter bearing aloft a chocolate cake with thirteen candles burning on it and a white skull and crossbones in the centre.'

It was a brave gesture. Interesting to relate, no fatalities resulted. Indeed the only bad luck at the banquet was the spilling of a tureen of hot soup over the heads of some of the diners.

DREAMS

Just as those who claim that fortune or fatality is contained in numbers, and just as there are those who read the signs of the heavens to predict future events, so one can find people who interpret the workings of the unconscious mind for the same purpose. Dreams have even been regarded by the superstitious as predictions of what was about to happen. To a believer they were firm omens of coming events. It was generally believed that one dream was not to be noted much, but if the same dream was repeated three times then the dream was said most surely to come to pass. It is easy to dismiss this as nonsense and to place dream interpretation in the fun area of life, but deep in the hearts of many people lies the fear that there may be something in it. While they would not openly confess to this superstition, a particularly vivid dream leads them to ponder its meaning, in spite of the fact that Freud considered the analysis of dreams as the royal road to the understanding of the dynamics of the mind.

Many would claim dreams to be prophetic because it is proved from Bible narratives that they have a divine significance. Believers in the literal truth of the Old Testament especially might well claim that if God has guided his people in one age by dreams, why not in another? It is in the interpretation of dreams and their associated divination that superstition finds a rich breeding-area. A page from an old-fashioned dream book gives some idea of the scheme:

ALEHOUSE—If a female dreams she is in an alehouse, it is a sign that her future husband will love his cups.

ANGELS—For a woman to dream of two angels is an indication she will have twins the next birth.

BED—To dream of being in bed signifies a very early marriage to yourself; and to dream of making a bed indicates a change in residence, and that you will live from home a long time.

BEES—To dream of bees is good, it denotes that your industry and enterprise in trade will be very successful.

BEEF—To dream of eating beef indicates that you will always live in plenty, though you may not be rich.

CATS—An unfavourable dream, denoting treachery.

CLOVER—'I do not know a better dream than this,' says Ptolemy. If you are in love nothing can be more favourable, and all your undertakings will prosper.

EGGS—denote success in trade and love.

FAIRY—'To dream that you see a fairy,' says the ancient

astrologer Sergeius, 'is a very favourable dream'. Beggars have had this dream, and afterwards become very rich.

GOD—This is a dream which seldom occurs; it is principally confined to those who are afflicted, and those about to die. To the pious it denotes a happy death.

LION—This dream denotes greatness, future elevation.

MAY-POLE—If a widow dreams of dancing round a May-pole it foretells that she will marry again.

PARLIAMENT—To dream you are a visitor, and that you listen to the debates, foretells family quarrels and dissensions; also that you will quarrel with your sweetheart and friends.

TOMBS—To dream you are walking among tombs foretells marriages; to dream that you are ordering your own tomb denotes that you will shortly be married.

Dream analysis did not achieve respectability until Freud used it to supplant his 'free-association method' of psychoanalysis, to disclose the buried memories which underlie a patient's symptoms. It is nevertheless difficult to eradicate superstition which has its basis in the function of sleep over which human beings have little or no control. Only a complete understanding of the operation can alleviate the fears of the superstitious. To prohibit dreaming by legislation would be nonsensical, yet it is just as difficult to persuade people not to wonder about the meanings of their dreams.

CHAPTER EIGHT

Divination

THE RELIGIOUS call it Providence, the sceptic superstition. Whatever one's attitude, divination holds most of mankind in its thrall. It differs from astrology in that it is the deliberate searching out of a particular answer, as opposed to the simple interpretation of data already irrevocably decreed in the planets. The instrument of search differs also. Divination employs birds, dice, bones, and rods to provide its answers; the last named, in fact, is even in the scientific day of the late seventies of the twentieth century an established means of detecting underground springs. Water is itself a long founded element for divination, a relic which remains to the present day in the quaint eccentricity of 'reading tea leaves'.

Divination was believed to have the power to determine the truth as well as the future. In primitive society the practice of trial by water and fire to establish innocence or guilt was widespread. It was believed also, that man need not search incessantly for answers about his future: he possessed, he was taught, a guardian spirit or angel, which forewarned him in time of need by various means of homely communications such as bodily itching, or a sneeze.

IMPLEMENTS OF THE ART

Common to all mankind is the desire for knowledge, and the attempt to penetrate mysteries and to discover what the future holds in store is universal. This, veined with traces of fear and awe, together with the belief that gods from time to time communicated knowledge of the future to chosen individuals, led to the consulting of oracles and the practice of divination. Divination, this magical revelation, worked through the deductions made from examining signs which the gods sent, and privileged man to observe and they were to be found largely in the sacrifices offered to these gods. Cicero maintained that all nations believed in divination:

'To say the truth, superstition has spread among all peoples, and has captured almost every mind, taking advantage of human weakness. It is ever pursuing and driving us, whether a man listens to a prophet or an omen, whether he sacrifices a victim or catches sight of a bird of warning, whether he meets an Eastern soothsayer or an Italian inspector of entrails, whether he sees lightning or hears thunder, or finds an object struck' (Cicero—*De Divinatione*).

Such was man's avid dependence upon divination and such were some of the most common implements of the art.

The Greeks, when observing the flight of birds for the purpose of divination, turned their faces towards the north, and if a bird appeared to the east, especially an eagle, a heron or a falcon, it was considered to be a favourable sign; birds appearing to the west, however, were regarded as a bad omen.

Jupiter, prince of light, was the supreme deity of Roman mythology, and not only was he lord of heaven but he also controlled human life, and through the flights of birds and signs in the heavens he allowed man a glimpse into the future. One of the religious officials of Rome in the Roman Empire was the augur, who predicted future events from the flight of birds; he would mark out the sphere of the sky to be used for observations, and birds flying in the left of that sphere made the augury lucky: flying on the right, however, was considered ill-fated.

It is said that the ancient Druids took auguries from the varying note of the wren's call, and in some parts of England it was known as 'the devil's bird'. The most persistent superstition regarding birds in Britain, however, attaches to the magpie. A single magpie was one of the worst of evil omens, but when accompanied by others there was a different significance attached to each number.

> 'One for sorrow
>   Two for mirth,
>   Three for a wedding,
>   Four for a birth.
>   Five for rich

Six for poor,
Seven for a witch
I can tell you no more.'

If one had the misfortune to see a single magpie there were
various charms that were supposed to ward off the impending
sorrow. One was to greet it kindly, by raising one's hand or
dropping a curtsy; another, to make the sign of the cross on
one's breast or cross the thumbs.

An old Scandinavian superstition probably lingers on in the
innocent saying, 'A little bird told me', when one prevaricates
about the source of one's information. In Northern mythology
Huginn and Muninn were the two ravens, said to symbolise
memory and thought, who sat on the shoulders of the god
Odin. To understand in greater depth and definition the significance of messages conveyed by birds, the writer of *The
Boke of The Mervayles of the World*, offers this advice: 'If thou
wilt understand the voyces of birds, associate with two fellows
in the twenty-eighth day of October, and goe into a certaine
wood with dogges as to hunt. And cary home with thee the
beast which thou shalt find first. Prepare it with a heart of a
foxe, and thou shalt understand the voice of birds and beasts.
And if thou wilt also that any other understand, kisse him,
and he shall understand.' Thus one could become a skilled
interpreter of divine messages purveyed by avian agents.

So throughout man's history birds have been regarded as
messengers of the gods, and accordingly looked upon with awe
and respect. An obvious reason why they should be so regarded
would be sensibly deduced from the fact that they have wings
which can carry them high into the atmosphere and thus near
the climes inhabited by the gods. Might this factor have something to do with the development in our own twentieth century
of the thrill connected with UFOs? True, we have grown out
of the naïvety of believing in the gods of our forefathers. The
belief in a supernatural power—perhaps inhabiting another
planet—however, a power from the dimension of science
fiction—this belief is not scoffed at as naïve: on the contrary,
superstitious belief in these unidentified flying objects is rapidly
gaining support; and even in such a sophisticated continent as
the United States of America, devotion to and credibility in

these mysterious objects is steadily shaping into something of a religion in some quarters, people believing that they are sinisterly connected with visitors from outer space who appear from time to time as they survey the planet earth.

ODD LOTS

> 'Seven's my luck, and yours is five and three;
> God's blessed arms! If you play false with me
> I'll stab you with my dagger!' Overthrown
> By two small dice, two bitching bits of bone,
> Their fruit is perjury, rage and homicide.'
>
>   (Chaucer. *The Pardoner's Tale*)

To see a child playing a game of snakes and ladders with counters and dice is as innocently removed from the gambling vice of the gaming table, as either game of chance is, when compared with the original purpose of casting lots—to find out knowledge of future events. The lot had many forms, from the disk Urim and Thummim in the days of Saul, first King of Israel (1 Samuel 14.41f) to the wooden or bone counters used especially among the Italian nations from the third century BC onwards to seek out knowledge of fate concerning the person who drew the lot. These lots, or counters, having various messages or verses written upon them, were usually thrown into an urn of water, and whatever message was later drawn out was supposed, for the one who drew it, to be applicable for himself.

Sometimes these lots were actual bones, and a common means of divination practised in South Africa by such tribes as the Matebell and Basuto was that of 'throwing bones'. From this act were discovered such answers as the best sites for a homestead, or where to search for strayed cattle; and, as common to every age, like the lie detector of our own day, the identity of a thief. The bones appear to have been used in much the same way as cards are, nowadays, used by fortune-tellers.

A rather different method of employing bones to predict the future is found in the writings of Giraldus Cambrensis. He mentions the practice in Wales during the twelfth century and early thirteenth century of discovering past events and predicting the future by inspecting the right shoulder-bones of rams which had been boiled and not roasted. By examination of the cracks and marks on the bones, those skilled in the art could predict peace or war, slaughters and conflagrations, domestic infidelities, and the condition of the king.

In the sixteenth century diviners made predictions concerning the future from patterns made by earth which was first tossed into the air and allowed to fall on a flat surface. Geomancy, or earth prophecy, seems to have been closely associated with magic, since magic signs, figures and circles were all part of the process. Divination by arrows (belomancy) consisted in labels containing advice being attached to a given number of arrows. The advice contained on the arrow which travelled furthest was that which was taken. Akin to this was botanomancy—divination by leaves. After writing messages on the leaves they were then tossed to the winds. The answer was finally deduced by retrieving and then studying what was written on those leaves which had been left behind.

Divination by the cockerel was carried out thus: a circle was drawn on the ground, the letters of the alphabet being written within it and a grain of corn being placed upon each letter. Next, a cock was turned loose in the circle and allowed to peck up the corn as he would. A record was made of the letters uncovered and from these the answer was calculated. This form of divination was termed alectryomancy.

Less contrived was the superstition in Classical Greek times which employed the notion that when a person fell into trance the soul left the body for the purpose of receiving divine revelation. The ancient Greeks had among them diviners who used this trance, *ekstasis* interpreting what they had seen while they were 'outside the body' as a message from the deity. Apropos this belief, there is a passage from Paul's second epistle to the Corinthians which bears a striking comparison: 'I knew such a man, (whether in the body, or out of the body I cannot tell: God knoweth.) How that he was caught up into paradise, and heard unspeakable words, which it is not lawful for a man to utter' (2 Cor. 12.2–4).

The methods of divination are legion. Besides these we have observed here, there are others which range from pouring melted lead into water, repeating incantations, throwing stones at a mark, revolving a key over a Bible, swinging a pendulum, even spinning a coconut.

Comprehensive are those types of divination found recorded in Holy Scripture such as dreams and their interpretation, in which Joseph, eleventh son of Israel was so adept, as recorded in Genesis. Then there was the casting of lots, as employed in the division of territory among the Israelites when they settled in Canaan; and the lots cast in the New Testament for a successor to Judas Iscariot when 'the lot fell upon Matthias'. The first book of Samuel, chapter 28, makes mention of witchcraft and necromancy—practices which, although he had banned them, King Saul became pressed by fear to resort to, as indeed he did with the prophetic breastplate which the high priest wore. All through his reign, in fact, Saul showed tentencies towards superstitious belief, perhaps because of 'the evil spirit' which, we read, tormented him from time to time. And almost every time he sought help of these means, Samuel was there and rebuked him (I Sam. 15.23).

In the fourth chapter of the book of Hosea, verse 12, we find evidence of rhabdomancy, or the use of the divining-rod; and in Ezekiel, 21,21 we find hepatoscopy, that is the inspection of animal's livers to discover the gods' will. The book of Daniel with its dreams and visions tells us of judicial astrology in the court of Nebuchadnezzar, King of Babylon (Dan. 2.2), a form of seeking divine revelation common in Egypt also (Gen. 41.8).

Household gods or teraphim feature in the Old Testament as well, a very human occurrence of which occurs in Genesis 31 when Rachel stole her father Laban's idols and set him to fruitless trouble finding them.

WORDS OF WARNING

Divination by words is of ancient origin, and was used both in Rome and Greece. The practice of opening some book of poems at random, and accepting the passage which turned up as an answer, probably arose from the esteem in which poets were held as divine and inspired persons. Among the Romans Virgil had most credit, whilst among the Greeks the works of Euripides and Homer were favoured. Street 'lots', or *sortes viales*, were also used in Greece and Rome. The person wishing to know his future carried a number of lots, on which were recorded certain characters or inscriptions. The first boy he met as he walked up and down the public highway was asked to draw from the lots, and the inscription recorded on it was regarded by the person as an infallible prophecy. Plutarch records that this method of divination was derived from the Egyptians, by whom the words and actions of young boys were regarded as containing in them something prophetical.

Writing on the effects of imagination, Bacon says: 'And, for words, there have been always, either barbarous ones, and of no signification, lest they should disturb the imagination; or words of similitude, to second and feed it; and this as well in heathen charms, as those of latter times. They also use Scripture words; for the belief that religious texts and words have power, and may strengthen the imagination. And for the same reason, Hebrew words, which with us, are accounted more Holy and mystical, are often used for this purpose.' It is probable that the Victorian habit of wearing a brooch inscribed *Mizpah* ('May the Lord watch between me and thee while we are apart') as a token of faith was a remnant of this tradition. Divination by the Bible, a practise still in existence in certain circles to this day, was condemned by the sixteenth canon of the Council of Vannes in AD 465, when the clergy were warned, under pain of excommunication, to desist from this superstitious practice. The prohibition was extended to the laity by the thirtieth canon of Orleans in 511, as it had been by preceding and subsequent councils, yet despite all this, it continued as a popular method of divination.

Sortes Sanctorum, or divinations by the Bible, although they were repeatedly condemned by the decrees of councils of the Church as tricks of divination of heathen origin, were repeatedly practised by the people, and even by kings, bishops and saints. One form of this superstition was to place on the altar or sacred tomb three different books of the Bible, for instance, the Prophets, The Acts of the Apostles, and Revelation. The consulter would then open one of the books at random and examine the exposed text for guidance and the prediction of future events.

An authority on the Cornish way of life, the Rev. R. S. Hawker, who died in 1875, told of the superstitious practice of elderly women who opened their bibles at random on New

Year's Eve to discover their luck for the coming year. 'A text on which the forefinger of the right hand rested was supposed to foretell the future.'

DOWSING

Many of us are familiar with the part which divining-rods played in ancient Egyptian history. During his pleas for Israel's freedom, Moses made no little use of his rod in attempts to dazzle Pharaoh Rameses II, and Exodus tells us that 'the magicians of Egypt did the same by their secret arts', and for a time matched these wonders. In the sixteenth century the divining-rod was employed in England to detect a murdered corpse. Similar to this is an account recorded in *The Gentleman's Magazine* of 8 February 1767, which states that: 'An inquisition was taken at Newbury, Berks, on the body of a child nearly two years old who fell into the river Kennet, and was drowned. The body was discovered by a very singular experiment. After diligent search had been made in the river for the child, to no purpose, a twopenny loaf, with a quantity of quicksilver put into it, was set floating from the place where it was supposed the child had fallen in, which loaf steered its course down the river for more than half a mile, before a great number of spectators, when the body happening to lie on the contrary side of the river, the loaf suddenly tacked about, and swam across the river, and gradually sank near the child, when both the child and the loaf were brought up, with grabbers ready for that purpose.'

In a broadcast on 9 January 1973 in the BBC programme 'Leap in the Dark', dealing with the para-normal, it was reported that diviners are used by the police force from time to time, and that the Gas Board and other commercial firms make use of dowsers. So, in an age when the occult has become fashionable, it is not surprising to hear as well that crystal balls, manufactured in Britain, are being exported to the United States.

In mining districts especially, there prevailed the superstition that some people were born gifted with an occult power of detecting the proximity of veins of metal, and of underground sources of water. The method of exercising this faculty was to cut a hazel twig just below where it forks. The divining-rod was then made by stripping off the leaves, cutting the two branches to about a foot in length leaving a three inch stump. The diviner then operated by tucking the elbows into his sides with forearms held horizontal, the branches being held in the hands, with the stump pointing forwards, the knuckles down, and the thumbs outwards. The diviner then walked over the area to be investigated, and as he passed over metal, or an underground spring, the hazel-fork jerked spontaneously in his hands. This, of course, parallels exactly the system used by water-diviners of today. Even in the sophisticated and scientific days of the late twentieth century, the divining-rod is still efficacious in discovering hidden water springs, and not only the superstitious-minded believe in them.

In pre-Christian times it was believed that every river had its presiding spirit; thus waters were used for divination as indeed were wells. This practice is carried into the present time by the adaptation of using the national drink. Thus in England tea-leaves are read, whereas in America coffee grounds are studied for the purpose of examining the future. The prediction is made from the arrangement of the tea-leaves or coffee grounds in the cup after the remaining liquid has been made to wash the sides of the vessel in a right-hand-turn direction and then been emptied. Prediction is also made by observing the direction in which the coffee bubbles rise in the cup; the superstitious believer gathers an indication whether or not wealth is to come his way. If the bubbles move towards him money will shortly be forthcoming; if they move away on the other hand, then money will be lost. In Macedonia, however, 'one solitary bubble in the centre of the cup betokens that the person holding it possesses one staunch and faithful friend. If there are several bubbles forming a ring close to the edge of the cup, they signify that he is fickle in his affections, and that his heart is divided between several objects of worship; and so forth' (Frazer, *Folk-Lore in the Old Testament*).

DISCOVERING THE TRUTH

Both divinations and ordeals were methods used in order to discover the truth. Divination was practised by a third party, whereas ordeal was undergone by the person accused to demonstrate his innocence. It was certainly in use in the North of

England in the sixteenth century. Dr Swift, Vicar-General and
Official Principal of the Diocese of Durham from 1561 to 1577,
recorded, 'A confession to be made by Alice Swan, wife of
Robert Swan, in S. Nicole's Church at Newcastle, for turning
the riddle (sieve) and shears, with certain others, after the
minister upon Sunday after the sermon.' It appears that the
practice of using a riddle and shears in this country for divination was superseded by the book (psalter or bible) and key.
In order to discover a thief, the key was placed on the fiftieth
psalm, the book closed, and fastened tightly with string. The
bible and key were then suspended to a nail and the name of
the suspected person was recited three times together with
these words:

> 'If it turn to thee,
> Thou art the thief and we are all free.'

A singular case of superstition revealed itself at the Borough
Petty Sessions at Ludlow on 7 January 1879. 'A married woman
named Mary Anne Collier was charged with using abusive and
insulting language to her neighbour Eliza Oliver; and the complainant in her statement to the magistrate, said that on
27 December she was engaged in carrying water, when Mrs
Collier stopped her, and stated that another neighbour had had
a sheet stolen, and had "turned the key on the Bible" *near
several houses*; that when it came to her (Collier's) house, the
key moved of itself, and that when the complainant's name
was mentioned, the key and the book turned completely round,
and fell out of their hands. Mary Anne Collier then asserted
that the owner of the sheet enquired from the key and the
Book whether the theft was committed at dark or at daylight,
and the reply was "Daylight." Defendant then called complainant a —— daylight thief, and charged her with stealing
the sheet. The Bench dismissed the case, the chief magistrate
expressing his astonishment that such superstition and ignorance should exist in the borough. It had been explained by
one who professed to believe in this mode of detecting thieves
that the key is placed over the open Bible at the words, "Whither
thou goest I will go" (Ruth 1.16); that the fingers of the
persons were held so as to form a cross, and the text being
repeated, and the suspected person named, the key then began

to jump and dance about with great violence, in such a way that no one could keep it still.' (*Birmingham Daily Post*, Jan. 10, 1879.)

BODY MALFUNCTION

There exists a body of superstitions which would appear to be based on the assumption that man has a spirit watching over him who forewarns him of future events. These supernatural guardians have various ways of making their presence felt and of communicating with their human charges. Thus the Dutch, like the English, believed that a tingling or itching ear was a sign that someone was speaking about you behind your back. Indeed, this superstition still holds. If the tingling appeared in the right ear you were being praised; if in the left, someone was speaking ill of you. On the other hand, if a tingling left ear so warned you, you could get your own back by biting your little finger, for it was believed that the evil speaker's tongue would suffer the identical fate.

To shudder involuntarily was believed to be an indication that someone was walking over the shudderer's grave, and the itching of the thumb was thought to signify the approach of some kind of evil power. So Shakespeare, in *Macbeth* IV.i wrote for the second witch:

'By the pricking of my thumbs,
Something wicked this way comes.'

For the palm of the right hand to itch, however, was a portent for the reception of a gift; and to rub the itching palm against wood was to make positively sure of its arrival:

'Rub it 'gainst wood,
'Tis sure to come good.'

In spite of the advances of modern medicine, the sneeze is still commonly assumed to indicate future events:

Sneeze on Monday, sneeze for danger,
Sneeze on Tuesday, kiss a stranger,
Sneeze on Wednesday, get a letter,
Sneeze on Thursday, something better,
Sneeze on Friday, sneeze for sorrow,
Saturday, see your true-love to-morrow.

A curious extension of this field of superstition developed in the days of transportation to the colonies. When this was the accepted punishment in England and offenders were banished, their families believed they could foretell their welfare and state of health by the condition of a sample of their urine which was kept in a bottle for this express purpose. Hung up in the home, it was studied from time to time, and should it become cloudy the exile's family knew he was suffering. If the urine remained clear they knew all was well; but should the urine evaporate and disappear from the bottle altogether, this was the worst possible omen and signified the person's death with dreadful certainty.

CHAPTER NINE

Holy Seasons and Weather

PERHAPS THE most vital element in life with which man has to contend is weather. He may take his choice as to believing in fate, the gods or the stars, but over the weather he has no option. At the same time, however, he is vitally dependent upon it, so it may be said that at the root of all weather superstition lies the urgent necessity to control or at least conciliate its powers since more than any other factor in life, it is weather which has the greatest effect upon man's ability to subsist. Superstition has evolved a number of methods for this beguilement: imitation of the weather desired, libations, the innocent aid of twins or toads, or simply the stern challenge of a strong man.

Besides being a general hazard with which to contend, weather could also affect mankind particularly, both benignly and with malevolence—factors which caused the growth of days of omen. Associated with fair days there seemed little more than the assurance of comeliness, grace, the joyful spirit or goodness, depending upon which day of the week a child was born, but with foul weather there has developed an abundance of 'signs', the most conspicuous causing misfortune, pestilence and death, and mentioning names like Julius Caesar, Judas Iscariot, Henry VIII and the ill-fated cities Sodom and Gomorrah.

Hard on the fringe of weather come the seasons and saints' days. Each of these bore some message for man, and all customs artlessly observed, whether at Christmas, Easter or St Swithin's Day, can be found to be grounded in the bedrock of superstition.

WEATHER-CONTROL

The desire to control the elements is common to all nations, all professions and classes, and all time. In our own generation, airlines are hampered by indissoluble fogs, communities are helplessly swept away in hurricanes or tidal waves, while others face famine because of drought. Sentimentalists pray for snow at Christmas, farmers for sunshine in July to ripen the harvest; gardeners and arthritics dread the frost, and mothers curse wet Saturdays. Thus for good reasons or not, throughout the generations of time, mankind has wished for control over the weather.

In Classical times the Romans and Greeks had their answers to these problems, for it is known that the priests of Apollo brought down lightning on the barbarians approaching the temple of Minerva, while the Greeks offered libations to Neptune in order to destroy the Persian fleet. Biblical evidence shows intriguing instances of the ability of the ancient Jews to call down fire from heaven to consume their burnt offerings. There is, besides the famous story of the prophets of Baal on Mount Carmel, the less well-known incident in 2 Kings I of the prophet of the Lord calling down fire on the king's captain and his fifty men. (The rebuke of Jesus to James and John in Luke 9.54, when they asked, 'Lord do you want us to bid fire come from heaven and consume them?' may be a significant indication of the Christian point of view concerning this practice.)

Not only was it fire that was called down; rain as well features in the Scriptures, while the rainmakers of India called down rain by setting their women, of whatever caste, to draw the plough through the parched fields during the hours of darkness.

The prophet Elijah earnestly prayed Yahweh for rain and waited long for the appearance of the 'small black cloud the size of a man's hand' to signal the imminence of the cloud-burst. There is also the nautical story in the Old Testament, (suspected by many sceptics to be 'fishy' in more than the literal sense), that of Jonah who was cast overboard in order to placate the gods and calm the storm. Seamen, indeed, are believed to be notoriously superstitious, and this idea of casting some sacrificial offering into the waters has a number of mani-festations, one of which was that a cat thrown into the sea would avert a tempest. This superstition had a counterpart, namely that to rouse up a tempest deliberately, a rag should be dipped into the water and beaten on a stone three times in the name of Satan:

'I knock this rag upon this stane,
To raise the wind in the devil's name!
It shall not lie till I please again.'

Mariners in the Middle Ages believed that whistling would produce a wind—a soft whistle for a breeze, a loud one for a gale—and vestiges of this superstition, or spell-casting upon the weather, remain to the present day in yachtsmen who 'whistle for a wind'. Alternatively, to scratch the mast or throw a coin into the sea would create similar effects. Hens' eggs, also, were potent aids in weather-control at sea. Their presence on board was supposed, some European sailors maintained, to produce contrary winds, whose only rectification was the wasteful act of throwing the eggs overboard.

In his novel, *The Pirate*, Sir Walter Scott writes about King Eric (also called Windy Cap), who could change the direction of the wind by turning his cap round on his head. Mention is also made of old Scots women who, for a consideration, would undertake to bring wind from any desired quarter. In the same novel, Norma of Fitful Head professed to control the wind by merely waving her wand in the air. Equally imposing as a weather wizard was King Mananan-bey-mac-y-Lheir who, tradition claims, ruled the Isle of Man during the fifth century in the Druid period. This monarch apparently required no weaponry for the protection of his kingdom, for on sighting a suspect ship approaching, he called down a fog and effectively concealed the island.

There are superstitions which still hold their ground even in the sceptical age of scientific observation. The St Swithin fallacy, for example, based on one remarkable coincidence, grew into a belief which lingers on in spite of all scientific evidence to the contrary:

'St Swithin's day, if thou dost rain,
For forty days it will remain:
St Swithin's day, if thou be fair,
For forty days 'twill na mair.'

The superstitious idea of forty days of rain after St Swithin's day may have originated in the story of Noah, when 'all the fountains of the great deep burst forth, and the windows of the heavens were opened. And rain fell upon the earth forty days and forty nights.' Yet the popular superstition concerning St Swithin's Day is founded on a legend that after the saint's canonisation, the monks of Winchester wished to translate his body from the common churchyard into the abbey chancel; but the solemn procession was delayed on 1 July and for forty days after by violent rains, which were supposed to have been produced by the humble-minded saint. Whatever the truth behind the theory, a certain fact to emerge from the St Swithin's myth is that some power or other appears amply competent in producing the temperate climate which prevails in the British Isles. Droughts of any severity and prolongation are generally confined to the tropical climes of the earth, chiefly central Australia, Africa and India.

In seasons of severe drought at Rudraganj in Bengal, the doors of the temple of the god Rudradeva were closed, and the precious offering of water was poured over the idol by Brahmins until it was immersed up to the chin. This practice was almost infallibly successful, though occasionally it happened that the element used to propitiate the god was blood. (Reminiscent of this is the evidence given us of the prophets of Baal slashing themselves with knives and lancets as they leapt frenziedly about their altar in attempts to attract the attention of their god.)

Another incident substantiating the idea of sacrifice being involved in man's pleading with the deity for water can be found in Bodinn's *Demonmania Pontanus*. He tells of a severe drought in Italy being dramatically relieved by the burial, in the portal of a church, of a live donkey which had first been given the consecrated host.

RAIN-MAKING
The general principle underlying the attempts by man to control the weather, however, was that he identified himself with the phenomenon he wished to produce and acted it out imitatively. So in drought Russian women would crowd down to rivers and bathe, having first doused the local pastor with pitchers of water; or the Javanese, having the problem, rather,

of too much rain, called upon the professional weather-doctor and begged him to extend his powers in stopping the rain; which operation he performed by abstaining from contact with water of any kind, whether for drinking or washing, and all the time seated in his room before an oil lamp, uttering incantations to the rain spirits beseeching them to return to their own country.

In some parts of Africa twins were believed to possess special powers for propitiating the gods for appropriate weather; and common in sorcery is the association of toads with water, so that amongst some peoples they are revered as gods of water, or by others, placed on hill tops, as near to the sky as possible, in an attempt to draw rain down to the parched earth.

A legend prevailed in Wales that in the mountainous regions of that land was a lake containing a path of stepping-stones. To pick one's way along them and successfully throw a handful of water as far as the very last stone was to ensure rain before nightfall.

Obviously, when man dabbles in superstitious ways of controlling the rainfall, the other equal element must be accounted for also: control of the sun. Regarded as a god by many primitive people, its favour was sought by various means largely based on sacrifice. It could be commanded, as when Joshua bade it, 'Sun, stand thou still, at Gibeon,' at which command the great orb halted miraculously, 'in the midst of heaven, and did not hasten to go down for about a whole day'; in the main, however, the sun was placated with offerings, sometimes human as in Mexico, often horses as in ancient Greece, for the Greeks believed the sun itself to be a charioteer. How better then than to sacrifice chariot and horses to him by drowning them in the sea whither the great god sun himself resorted every evening?

DAYS OF ILL OMEN

Such have been some of man's attempts at controlling the natural elements. One must next ask the question, to what extent do the elements and seasons affect man? The answer is quite simply, considerably. 'Somme wryte (their ground I see not) that Sondaye's thundre should brynge the death of learned men, judges, and others: Mondaye's thundre, the death of women: Tuesdaye's thundre, plentie of graine: Wednesdaye's thundre, the deaths of harlottes, and other blodshede: Thursdaye's thundre, plentie of shepe and corne: Fridaie's thundre, the slaughter of a great man, and other horrible murders: Saturdaye's thundre, a generall pestilent plague and great deathe' (Digges, *Prognosticacion Everlausting of ryght goode Effects*, 1596).

There was the similarly imposing jingle warning folk to beware of the perils of certain days in the calendar:

'First Monday in April, the day on which Cain was born, and Abel was slain; the second Monday in August, on which day Sodom and Gomorrah were destroyed; the 31st December, on which day Judas was born, who betrayed Christ; these are dangerous days to begin any business, fall sick, or undertake any journey.'

As far as wedding-days were concerned, superstition maintained,

> Monday for wealth,
> Tuesday for health,
> Wednesday the best day of all;
> Thursday for losses,
> Friday for crosses,
> And Saturday no luck at all.

We may not be particularly impressed by the superstition which marks these days of ill omen, but it is nevertheless true that even now many business people will refrain from starting any new enterprise on a Friday, especially if that day should be the thirteenth of the month.

In many instances this superstition relied on unpleasant associations connected with a particular day. In less enlightened times undue importance was attached to strange coincidences like those which marked the departure from this life of Henry VIII and his posterity, for they all died on a Tuesday; Henry VIII on Tuesday, 28 January 1547; Edward VI on Tuesday, 6 July 1553; Mary on Tuesday, 17 November, 1558; Elizabeth on Tuesday, 24 March, 1603 (John Booker). It was also considered unlucky to take medicine, to get married or to be bled on a Friday. And any child born on this day was doomed perpetually to misfortune. 'Her dreames are so chaste that she dare tell them'; wrote Sir Thomas Overbury, 'only a Fridaie's dreame is all her superstition; that she conceales for feare of anger' (*Character of a faire and happy Milkmaid*). To break an ornament on Good Friday, however, was very fortunate since the broken pieces were said to pierce the body of Judas Iscariot, the man who betrayed Christ.

There were most pedantic niceties about when, or not, to have a manicure; and to cut nails upon a Friday, or a Sunday, was accounted unlucky amongst the common people in many places. 'The set and statary times of pairing nail, and cutting hair, was thought by many a point of consideration, which was perhaps but the continuation of an ancient superstition. To the Roman it was piacular to pare their nails upon the nundinae, observed every ninth day, and was also feared by others on certain days of the week, according to that of Ausonius, Ungues Mercurio, barbam Jove, Cypride crines' (Sir Thomas Browne). As for cutting one's nails on a Sunday, 'A man had better ne'er been born as have his nail on a Sunday shorn.'

Unless it were a foreshadowing of the Victorians' hypocritical misunderstanding of the command to rest on one day out of seven, (and whose rigid censure of such peccadilloes as reading light literature and sewing on buttons on Sunday made a farce of the injunction), it is hard to suggest a sensible reason for this warning. It is certainly known, however, that saints' days and holy days did not always bring the good fortune one might expect. In Caernarvonshire, near Bangor, there was a slate quarry owned by one of the landed gentry, Lord Penrhyn, whose workers always met with some catastrophe or other on Ascension Day. Rational explanations were made that it was all coincidence, and so after discussion, but yet with misgivings, it was agreed to carry on quarrying as though nothing had happened. Uncannily, nevertheless, the jinx persisted; each Ascension Day that the men worked one of them met with an accident, so that ultimately, reasoning or no, nothing would induce a man to sign on for blasting on that day.

CHRISTMAS

It is indeed a curious enigma that superstition insinuates itself into Christian seasons, and none in the Western world is so interwoven with such notions and practices as Christmas. On Christmas Eve in the year 1652 Parliament issued an order banning even the acknowledgement of Christmas Day. 'No observations shall be had of the five and twentieth day of December, commonly called Christmas Day; nor any solemnity used or exercised in churches upon that day in respect thereof,' but it did no good; the common practices were already too deeply grounded. The Druids had long since seen to it that Christmas was rightly a time for rejoicing and had appropriately exploited all opportunities. In return for a small offering they gave people sprays of consecrated mistletoe to ensure that their coming year should be happy. With the flair of the twentieth century's most persuasive advertising, 'Yule' was proclaimed! Yule logs for the fire's blaze, a Yule candle to bring starry brightness to the table, the Yule cake to accompany spiced ale and mince pies for the company's inner comfort.

True, these Christmas ingredients could be traced quite clearly to their origins, the spices of Christmas fare to call to mind the costly gifts of gold, frankincense and myrrh from the East; the star to light folk to the Christ child, and the burning logs, symbol of that light which came into the world, which light shined in the darkness. The name 'Yule' in fact, is said to derive from the Hebrew word 'lail' or 'lailah' 'night', so it may be seen how appropriately it complements the Christian symbols of light.

The idea would also, coincidentally, dovetail with the ancient Scandinavian festival begun at the winter solstice in honour of Thor. Associating the longest night of the year with creation, when the earth was formed out of darkness, they called it Mother-Night, and this festival of pagan worship was termed Yule or Yeol.

No Christmas nowadays is complete without the Christmas-tree. That the tree at Christmas is a custom of great antiquity there can be no doubt: plants and lights have been associated with the Winter Festival in all countries long before Christian times. One of the first mentions of the Christmas-tree in modern times occurs in a work called *The Milk of Catechism* published about the middle of the seventeenth century by Dr Johann Konrad Dannhauer of Strasbourg cathedral. He describes how people set up in their houses 'the Christmas- or fir-tree, hang with dolls and sweets, and afterwards shake and deflower.'

It is suggested that the Christmas-tree was a Protestant

rather than a Catholic institution and that it made only slow progress in those parts of Germany which still clung to the older faith. It first came into fashion in Germany in Luther's day; and it was the Prince Consort of Victoria, Albert, who encouraged its use in England, whence it spread over the European Continent and across the Atlantic to America. It was this country which instituted its use for the first time in churches as a central feature in religious services. The tree, as well, may be traced back to scriptural foundations according to some opinion: the trunk to symbolise the stem of Jesse, growing up through the human genealogy of Jesus, until at the top of the fir tree there is the star to represent the Christ child.

Presents and Santa Claus must join the festive throng, and these may be variously traced back. Santa Claus, of course, is well known as St Nicholas and, introduced to Britain in the latter eighteenth century, his hallmark was the secrecy with which he distributed his gifts. Gifts in Russia were credited to the Babuska, the Grandmother, a legendary old crone who was said deliberately to have misdirected the wise men from the East when they asked her the way to the child Jesus: repenting of the lie, however, she made amends by devoting all her time from then on to lavishing gifts on good children.

One of the rarer, wistful beliefs about Christmas to emerge into folklore is that of the American Indians who came under the influence of the Christian missionaries: hearing that the cattle had knelt on Christmas night to honour the Christ child, they claimed that the deer knelt also, to worship the Great Spirit; while the patron saint of animals, Francis of Assisi, maintained that Christmas was the time when all oxen and asses should be given extra provender 'for the reverence they showed the Son of God.'

PEACE PARASITE

In view of the fact that the Druids were wont to lavish sprays of consecrated mistletoe on people at Christmas, it would seem a paradox that it is shunned in Churches as a decoration. One exception only seems apparent—York Minster. There it was customary for a priest to lay a bunch of mistletoe on the altar. Stukeley writes, 'Lately at York, on the eve of Christmas Day, they carried mistletoe to the high altar of the Cathedral, and proclaimed a public and universal liberty, pardon, and freedom to all sorts of inferior and even wicked people at the gates of the city, towards the four quarters of heaven.'

Might it be intriguingly conjectured that, at the Minster, this plant was seen as a symbol of the mysterious virgin birth because of its extraordinary parasitical growth? The Swedish name for mistletoe is 'donnerbesen', the thunder blossom. In Scandinavia enemies met under the mistletoe if they wished to be reconciled, when they gave each other the kiss of peace; and it was sacred to the Norsemen as it was to the Druids. In Druidic rites it was always gathered with ceremony and used to be accompanied by sacrifice on certain nights of the year. Country people have always considered it unlucky to allow mistletoe to touch the ground or to cut down the tree on which it grows, believing it to be sacred and potent as a healer; and indeed the old name for mistletoe was 'All-Heal'.

In Ancient Norse mythology there is a legend which tells how Baldur the god of Summer Sun was invulnerable to any harm either from, on, or under the earth, but his cunning enemy Loki, observing the peculiarity of the mistletoe's growth, neither on nor under the earth, but in a tree, tipped his spear with mistletoe and killed Baldur. Freyja, however, the Goddess of Love, restored him to life, and the tears she had shed for him became the fruit of the mistletoe. To carry a twig of this plant about one's person was believed to protect one from the evil powers of witchcraft, and in some instances to facilitate communication with spirits. When mistletoe was found growing from an oak tree it was doubly sacred, and after the sacrifice of a white ox, it was carefully cut away by an Arch Druid using a golden knife, when great pains were taken to ensure it did not touch the ground lest it be contaminated and lose its sacredness.

NEW DAYS FOR OLD

Most pungent superstitions are associated with the fading old year and the rising new one. In the cold north it was believed to be a time of prowling witches, ghosts and hobgoblins; trolls were said to ride abroad on grizzly bears and werewolves, and the spine-chilling howls of mysterious beings blew in the winter gales. In some of the Scandinavian countries the notion prevailed that the family dead revisited the old home during this season, and frightened folk were bound to have a meal prepared for the ghosts on Christmas Eve, and even their beds, for these ancestral spirits demanded soft-feathered luxury, leaving their terrified relatives gratefully huddled in outhouse straw.

There used to be a time when the French, too, dreaded Christmas Eve, bolting every door and putting their beasts into shelter. For that was the night Satan walked abroad sending his witches and dwarfs, warlocks and the ghosts of suicides to roam the earth and terrorise mankind. Only the oxen and asses might be left in safety, for having seen the Holy Child's Nativity, they were immune from any sorcery.

Omens pervaded almost all beginnings. It was obvious therefore that New Year featured prominently:

'If New Year's Day, in the morning, open with dusky red clouds, it denotes strife and debates among great ones, and many robberies to happen that year' (Thomas Passenger. *The Shepherd's Kalendar*).

New Year's Day also set the year off to a bad start if a woman was the first to enter a house: or it might, just as unfortunately, be a red haired person. Since tradition maintained that Judas and Cain both had red hair, great suspicion fell on any whose colouring this was. Dark-haired people, on the other hand, were very happily acceptable, for the fortune they unwittingly brought and favours were lavished on them. Other ill-fated and ominous people were the flat-footed: called 'first foot', they were believed to bring ill luck since no water could run under their feet. Women were particularly unwelcome because of notions that they were endowed with prophetic powers, and among the ancient Scots, if a bare-footed woman crossed a road in front of them, they seized her and drew blood from her forehead, as a charm against the omen. Primitive Christians did little to stop this superstition since they designated the fair sex as 'Gates of the Devil, resigners of the Tree of Life, and the first deserters of the Divine Law' (Tertullian).

Just as Ascension Day was unlucky for some, as St Paul's Day, 25 January, marked the year's fortune-teller, and St Mark's Day the prognosticator of life and death, so another curious day—perhaps the most curious of all—is the first of

April, All Fools' Day. No certain origin or explanation is offered, yet many countries take advantage of the unsuspecting on that date. Scotland perhaps takes April fooling more seriously than Ireland or England. The old custom of 'hunting the gowk' (cuckoo) has its modern counter-part, and the day is still—as all Scots know—named 'Hunty Gowk'. It was once the custom to seize upon the simplest soul in the community and despatch him on a two-mile walk with a note for some other man. The other, on opening the note, saw written:

> 'This is the First of April,
> Hunt the Gowk another mile.'

He then promptly sent the messenger on with a similar note.

It is at the end of March in Japan that the gullible are confirmed for what they are. In China people send one another on absurd errands. In Denmark it is customary to 'send or run into April'; and the same tomfoolery applies equally in India where the Hindu festival of Huli ends on 1 April. 'During the Huli,' wrote Pearce in *Asiatic Researches*, 'when mirth and festivity reign, among the Hindus of every class, one subject of diversion was to send people on errands and expeditions that ended in disappointment and raised a laugh at the expense of the person sent.'

A German, in explanation, blamed the fickle April weather:

> 'April weather mocks you though!
> Rain or sunshine, clouds or snow.
> Sure of it you'll never be—
> April makes a fool of thee.'

Whatever the origin of these customs, it seemed sensible to attribute such hilarity to a nature feast, that of the vernal equinox, and to dedicate such behaviour to Maya, goddess of deception and illusion.

A similar idea prevailed in Belgium and France where the people were bidden to beware of the 'poissons d'Avril'. But in this case, the basis of the wariness was for a more sober reason, for some claimed that 'poissons' was a corrupted form of 'Passion', referring to the Passion of Jesus which took place when he was sent from Annas to Caiaphas, from Caiaphas to Pilate, from Pilate to Herod, and back to Pilate again; back-

wards and forwards, to and fro, the while tormented and
mocked.

So the holy seasons come full circle to the most holy of all,
the crucifixion, death and resurrection of Jesus Christ, the
bursting forth of dry grain into the green blade of new life.

It is interesting to speculate on the possible connection with
this idea that the originators of the Good Friday 'healing
bread' might have considered. Certainly bread baked on this
solemn day was significant because, when kept and later grated
into hot water, it supposedly provided healing and renewal of
strength. The hot cross bun, also, might have similar associations. Originally, however, it was simply a bun, the cross
being added by the early Christians to incorporate this token
of the pagan spring festival into the Easter feast of Christ. In
substance the bun was made of flour and honey, was a sacred
bread offered to the gods and was called 'Bonn' or 'Bous' as
the Greeks sometimes preferred to call it. In some descriptions
it would appear it was a cake with two horns. Not only was its
existence known to the Greeks; the Hebrew prophet Jeremiah
was aware of it. Imprisoned in Egypt, he condemned his fellow
countrymen and their wives for philandering with the idolatrous
customs of the Egyptians, and when the Jewish women retorted
petulantly that it meant nothing more than a social courtesy
making these 'crescent cakes marked with the image of the
Queen of Heaven', the man of God rebuked them bluntly for
apostasy. It is sad to reflect that, in spite of being later hallowed with the cross, the hot cross bun of the latter twentieth
century is no longer a symbol of a crucified God, but once
more a mere social habit. Other Good Friday superstitions that
developed were more overt in their connections with the
crucifixion; blacksmiths refused to work on Good Friday because hammer and nails were so cruelly instrumental in Christ's
death. Neither would gypsies touch water on that day. It was
with an innocent bowl of water, they argued, that Pontius
Pilate condemned himself when he washed his hands of the
King of the Jews.

In the churches of Florence in Italy, boys are permitted the
liberty of beating the benches with willows to enact the
'thrashing of Judas Iscariot'. And gardeners, ever optimists in
their dependence upon nature's seasons, believe it essential to

take advantage of such a holy day to ensure healthy crops.
New life after death, the grey winter followed by the vibrant
spring. Spring-cleaning in the home, spring bonnets in church:

> 'Last Easter I put on my blue
> Frockcoat, the vurst time, vier new;
> Wi' yaller buttons aal o' brass,
> That glittered in the zun like glass,
> Bekaze 'twer Easter Zunday.'

wrote the Dorset poet, William Barnes.

It was in fact once believed that the sun did actually dance
for joy when it rose on an Easter dawn in celebration of Christ's
rising from the dead. In Lincolnshire there used to be a custom
called the Wading of the Sun; on Easter Sunday morning at
sunrise a bucket of water was placed where it would catch the
first rays of the sun, and if the light trembled in the water the
season would be wet, but if it was steady then a fine year was
predicted.

An extraordinary custom emerged in the Middle Ages: set
properly in church and at worship, the mind was astonished to
learn that in this solemn setting, a kind of football became part
of the Easter celebration, and bishops, priests and choirboys
alike would all join heartily in the game. The priest would toss
the ball to a chorister who, in his turn, would toss it to another,
and so on, until all the officiating clergy and choristers had taken
part in the sedate game. Their game over, the players would
gather for a meal. The important dishes at these feasts were
huge gammons of bacon and tansy pudding, the latter being a
highly spiced dish, the herbs and ingredients of which represented the bitter herbs used at the Passover, in accordance
with the Jewish law.

It is appropriate: the Passover preceded the great eruption
into life of the Jewish nation; Good Friday was the last fetter
to be severed in the breaking out of new life, the Resurrection.
It is a time of miracles and wonders.

CHAPTER TEN

Health and Strength

BUT FOR the sneeze which was once regarded as a portent of death, the tenor of superstition surrounding healing is one of optimistic trust, and makes a refreshing change from the usual preponderance of gloomy wariness. The prime element in healing was water which, because of its great efficacy, became recognised universally, not least in the Christian Church. Thus developed the holy wells, and thence, pilgrimage. This devout journey, however, degenerated with use, and the healing holy water was joined by all manner of offerings made by pilgrims for cures desired and effected, so that the Church was compelled to curb the whole system and regularise pilgrimage with the plain symbol of the cockleshell; though in time even this got out of hand in its constant use by erring humanity.

Long before Christianity was established, however, and alongside water, there was the curative charm, the amulet. In form, the variety of these healing aids was legion, ranging from the ancient brass crescent to the mystical word charm 'Abracadabra'. On the way there were included 'mad' stones, the Lee Penny, dolls, feathers, the King's 'hand', the teeth and other parts of wild beasts and corpses, and even cakes filled with biblical texts. There was, besides, spittle. A valid enough substance for certain cures on rational grounds, it has, always been endowed with that enigmatic supernatural power ascribed to that other healing enigma, 'the seventh son'.

CURIOUS CURES

From time to time since man began to notice such curiosities, there has arisen the phenomenon of 'the seventh son of a seventh son'. Such men, it seems, are born with an uncanny gift to cure disease, and no explanation can be found for it. In the mid-twentieth century an Irish woman gave birth to her seventh son, and knowing of this phenomenon and also that her husband was born after six brothers, she placed a worm in her baby son's hand. 'It died,' she commented simply, 'so I knew my son would be a healer.' And so it transpired. What is the reason for this, one may ask? And what other unfathomable healing aids can there be found in the world? To the first question there is no answer; to the second one must reply that man has discovered a very great number, and all for the simple reason that there are countless numbers of ills in the world that cry out for relief and cure.

One of the great fundamental healing elements in the world is water. In the time of the patriarchs and their fellow Middle Eastern peoples, springs, wells and rivers were all significant because their movement, and life-giving power in the desert terrain gave them vitality and indeed supernatural qualities. So it was understandable that Jacob should wrestle with a spirit at the ford Jabbok, since such beings inhabited water.

Water could also heal. 'Dip in the Jordan seven times and be cured of your leprosy,' Naaman the Syrian was ordered. Later on we read, in the gospels, of the healing properties of the pool of Siloam. Indeed Baptism, while properly acknowledged as a mark of adoption into the Christian family and therefore a spiritual symbol, is still relied upon by old rooted country-folk to benefit more than simply the child's soul. Looking at a sickly baby, an old grandmother may even now say, 'Get him baptised, that'll make him come along all right.' More so-phisticated people might call that credulous, yet for all that would themselves, nonetheless, bring a bottle of Jordan water to church for their child's baptism.

When Christianity came to Britain, it found the native Celtic peoples thoroughly embedded in pagan beliefs; and featuring prominently in these beliefs was this same faith in water that appears common universally. Mindful of the part water played in their own faith and realising people's great trust in it, Christian believers wisely incorporated these holy places into their structure, and by dedicating wells and sacred spots to saints and endowing them with saintly healing powers, they succeeded in taking over the dwelling-places of heathen nymphs and Druidic spirits. Thus in Chester an altar was discovered inscribed on two sides with, 'Nymphis et Fontibus,' and, near it, the site of a well where various objects, vases, coins and the like had been thrown in, probably for magical purposes, or as propitiations to the presiding spirit of the water. In stark contrast, there once existed near Colwyn Bay in North Wales a well dedicated to St Elian which was thought to be a cursing well. Anyone wishing a curse to be laid on a person simply wrote the recipient's name on a small stone and dropped it into the water: the result of this action was, it was believed, to afflict the unfortunate victim with cramp, poverty, and even bereave him of his very life. Not at all sinister, and very reminiscent of present-day practices of throwing coins or pins into fountains, was the custom in parts of Bohemia of throwing into wells some of their Christmas fare as an offering to the water divinities in order to gain protection against drought the following year.

Most beliefs involving the power of water, however, were related to its curative or protective propensities for man. Thus, sanctified baptismal water was most beneficial for eye afflictions, or as a preventive against witchcraft. Yet let it be repeated, the basic power was in the natural substance of water: Christian hallowing was not essential.

In South Wales, not far from Kidwelly, the water of a most sinister gorge, steep and overgrown, which runs down to a tiny trickle of water coming out of a hill, is still a most potent healer. At the turn of the century, miners on their return from the pithead would make their perilous and fearful way down to it (for Ffynon Wil Water was both precipitous and eerie), in order to have sprains and dislocations cured. To apply the icy water to the affected part caused a savage burning and afterwards healing. A sceptic struggled down to the stream lately, defying it to have any effect on his injured neck, and was astonished to admit his scepticism dispelled.

Watering-places and spas, so popular fifty years ago, have slipped into a somewhat redundant gentility nowadays, though to stop off and drink some of the panacetic spa water is still a novelty. There is also, of course, the scientific substance given to such water which makes belief in its efficiency more rational. But such waters are different from those of Siloam or Madern's Well. Situated in Cornwall, this well was noted for its healing powers, and Bishop Hall of Exeter in *The Mystery of Godliness* wrote of it that 'in the miraculous cure which at Madern's Well was wrought on a poor cripple, I found neither art nor collusion the cure done there, the author an invisible God'.

PILGRIMAGE

Where such water was found, there were found also the sick thronging its banks in search of relief. Thus developed a branch of pilgrimage. Pilgrimage has had different purposes down the generations. To some it was a journey of penance emulating the hardships of past pilgrims. More recently it has become a progress of visits to shrines to commemorate and identify with those holy treks of ancient time. And continuing alongside its other purposes, the journey was taken to a holy place with the hope of cure.

Together with the pilgrim's belief and hope went a votive offering for the favour received. A letter of Margaret Paston dated 28 September 1443 explained that votive offerings were hung in venerated sanctuaries. 'If on the one hand, by striking a wax image together with appropriate incantations, someone might do you great harm, on the other, by placing your image in the chapel of a saint, great favours might be won and especially cures in cases of sickness.' There were also the quaint votive offerings made in true Irish style instanced by Carleton in his *Traits and Stories of the Irish Peasantry*:

'To St. Columbkill—I offer up this button, a bit o' the waist-band o' my own breeches, an' a taste o' my wife's petticoat, in reminbrance of us havin' made this holy station; an' may they rise up in glory to prove it for us in the last day.'

Such homespun offerings, together with other developments and results of pilgrimages, brought the whole conception into disrepute. Pilgrimages were discarded by the Church of England at the Reformation as being 'fond things vainly invented, grounded upon no warranty in Holy Scripture.' A quotation from *The Book of the Knight of La Tour Landry*, a French book of the fourteenth century edited by Thomas Wright in 1868, described how 'Places of pilgrimage were strewn with the crutches of cripples, swords of warriors, prisoners' irons, wax tablets, jewels and precious stones of all sorts.' At Rocamadour, so one can gather, tresses of women's hair were strung up as an admonition. They were, relates the Knight of La Tour Landry, those of 'ladies and gentille women that had be wasshe in wyne, and in other thinges for to make the here of colour otherwise thanne God made it, the whiche ladies and gentille women that aught (owned) the tresses were comynge thedirward on pilgrimage, but they may neuer haue powere to come withinne the chirche dore vnto the tyme that thei hadde cutte of the tresses of her here.'

Topped by some items from travelling notes kept by French pilgrims who made mention of such macabre sensations to be found in Venice as an ear of St Paul, the arm of St George, and even the 'whole roasted flesh of St Laurence turned to powder,' (also the inclusion of the molar teeth of Goliath) the whole reverence and solemnity of pilgrimage was tilted out of balance and its state reduced to one reminiscent of a peep-show.

Nonetheless out of its smelting pot there came one durable symbol of pilgrims which has endured through time and is still recognised as such: the cockleshell. This was the badge worn by pilgrims, which after being blessed by a priest was regarded as an amulet which protected the wearer from spiritual foes.

SUSPENDED CURES

Amulets were worn strung round the neck or tied about any part of the body for the purpose of warding off evil and securing advantages of some kind. The amulet consisted of a stone, plant or piece of writing which had some special significance for the wearer; and the word itself, 'hamalet', comes from the Arabic meaning 'that which is suspended'.

One of the most common parallels to be found in England is the horse brass: of different shapes, but often a crescent because of its origin in oriental moon-worship, these brasses were fixed on cart horse harness in order to ward off the evil eye. Even at the time of Israel's infiltration into Canaan, however, they were known. Gideon, having put to death the two Midianite kings, 'took the crescents that were about the necks of their camels.' Such amulets were part of a woman's finery also and were fiercely denounced by the prophet Isaiah (Isa. 3.18f), whose warnings to those who decked themselves with such charms was uncompromising.

An amulet which was extensively used in mediaeval times consisted of five Latin words arranged so that they could be read not only backwards and forwards, but up and down as well. In appearance they formed a block thus:

```
S   A   T   O   R
A   R   E   P   O
T   E   N   E   T
O   P   E   R   A
R   O   T   A   S
```

and the words stood for the Sower, the Plough, Words, Works, and Wheels. These cleverly woven letters impressed people as a magic formula and were, so evidence suggests, particularly efficacious in speeding up a difficult delivery at childbirth.

A graveyard was a regular treasure-chest of charms and talismans, and Sir Thomas Browne claims that the 'Bones, hairs, nails and teeth, of the dead were the treasures of old sorcerers'.

In primitive parts of Africa the same tools of the trade pertained: the hoof of a kid, the horn of a small antelope, shells, hair switches and the tooth of a leopard. Each was a certain cure for some malady or other. And even in supposedly less primitive Europe corresponding remedies were not dissimilar: rheumatism was thought to be relieved by wearing a ring made of three nails taken from a coffin in three different churchyards; toothache, by carrying in one's pocket the tooth of a corpse of the opposite sex; while a cure for whooping-cough was a necklace made of small twigs from elder-trees growing in a churchyard.

This superstitious belief in amulets as curative charms was carried to illegal lengths: a woman suffering from sore breasts could be relieved by despatching her husband to church at midnight on the errand of removing some lead from the window lattices out of which he had to fashion a heart-shaped amulet which was afterwards presented to the afflicted lady.

Beside lead hearts, there were cramp rings. Supplied by nine young men, the rings were made out of nine crooked sixpences and given to any young woman who admitted to attacks of epilepsy. Some believers in this superstition carried the operation out on a scale both lavish and complex. From *The Times* of 7 March 1854 we read, 'A young woman living in the neighbourhood of Halsworthy, North Devon, having for some time past been subject to periodical fits of illness, endeavoured to effect a cure by attendance at the afternoon service at the parish church, accompanied by thirty young men, her near neighbours. Service over, she sat in the porch of the church, and each of the young men as they passed out in succession, dropped a penny into her lap; but the last, instead of a penny, gave her half-a-crown, taking from her the twenty-nine pennies. With this half-crown in hand, she walked three times round the Communion table, and afterwards had the coin made into a ring, by the wearing of which she believed she would recover her health.'

Even more extraordinary is an extract from the *Japan Daily Herald* which on 26 November 1877 read, 'In order to escape cholera, the dogs in the Matsushima and neighbourhood, the cats and birds in Horiye, the monkeys and bears in Namba-jinchi, the rabbits in the Temma Temple and the deer in the Sakuranomiya Temple, are wearing charms.'

But perhaps the zenith of credulity was achieved in an account recorded in the *Boston Journal of Chemistry* in 1879. It appeared that a superstitious Texan who had a phobia of mad dogs, snakes and venomous reptiles in general had been told that to procure a 'mad' stone—the stone removed from the stomach of a deer some years before—would solve all his fears and in any case neutralise the poison should he be molested by any of the creatures he so dreaded. Such a charm he diligently sought out, and gladly paid out two hundred and fifty dollars for its possession.

A charm which possessed curative power and was given official sanction by the Presbyterian Church of Scotland was the Lee Penny. A small dark-red heart-shaped stone, it was set into the reverse side of an Edward IV groat and had a world-wide reputation. After due examination the Glasgow Synod recorded its findings, namely that 'without using onie words such as charmers and sorcerers use in their lawfull practises; and considering that in nature there are mony things seen to work strange effects, whereof no human witt can give a reason, it having pleasit God to give to stones and herbes special virtues for the healing of mony infirmities in man and beast, advises the brethren to surcease their process, as wherein they perceive no ground of offence; And admonishes the said Laird of Lee, in the using of the said stone, to tak heed that it be used hereafter with the least scandal that possiblie may be' (Simpson—*Proceedings of Society of Antiquities of Scotland*).

Such was the privilege of the Lee Penny that, when in the reign of Charles I the plague attacked the town of Newcastle, the inhabitants were prepared to pay £6,000 for its loan.

CHARMS AND SPELLS

It was, in fact, partly due to the Church's teaching on disease that superstition flourished so verdantly. Insisting that all maladies were a punishment from God, orthodox medical men were not given very much encouragement; indeed their attempts to alleviate sickness were interpreted as interference by the devil. This, of course, left the field wide open for magical practices where healing was concerned, and many cures involved the use of the most revolting ingredients as well as the muttering of secret charms. These charms and spells were placed in two classes—those which cured illness and those directed against evil such as witchcraft. During the great plague of London, Daniel De Foe made an inventory of the more common charms used to ward off the disease. Besides philtres, exorcisims and amulets, some wore the Jesuits' mark, ISH on a cross, while others put their trust in the signs of the zodiac. Very popular indeed was the magically efficacious word 'Abracadabra'. Today its power is limited almost entirely to use by conjurors at children's parties, yet in the 1500s it was powerful not only against the dreaded plague, but even for such trivial ailments as toothache and warts.

'Abracadabra' was worn in several ways for protection, basically, however, written as a triangle and suspended round the neck.

```
A B R A C A D A B R A
A B R A C A D A B R
A B R A C A D A B
A B R A C A D A
A B R A C A D
A B R A C A
A B R A C
A B R A
A B R
A B
A
```

The name appears to have originated from two sources. Some opinions tend to the belief that it was the name of a Syrian god whose aid was thought to be invoked by the wearer of the amulet. Others believed it to be a word made up from the initials of Hebrew and Aramaic words meaning Father, Son and Spirit. Philologically this is a plausible conjecture:

Abh, father; bar, son; and ruaḥ, spirit.

There is a danger of causing confusion when substantiating superstitious practices with parallels found in Scripture. The question may justifiably be asked, 'Where does faith end and superstition begin?' This danger was foreseen by the early Christian pioneers who overcame it in various ways; sometimes they took over the pagan ritual and 'Christianised' it (as with the sacred wells), or else they roundly condemned the adulteration of things holy. It was with this in mind that in *Burnynge of St Paule's Church*, Pilkington, in 1561, admonished his people: 'What wicked blindness is this then, to thinke that wearing prayers written in rolles about with theym, as St. John's Gospell, the length of our Lord, the measure of our Lady, or other like, thi shall die no sodain death, nor be hanged, or yf he be hanged, he shall not die.'

In spite of such stern censures, however, people continued to adulterate the gospel with misunderstanding and misuse. As protection from the wiles of the Devil cakes were used having an imprint of a lamb carrying a flag on one side and the head of Christ on the other. In the cake was placed a piece of paper or parchment containing texts from St John's Gospel. Known as the Agnus Dei, this charm was similar to the hot cross buns which were kept from one Good Friday to the next as a preventive against sickness.

The wild Irish were culpable as well. Hanging about their children's necks the beginning of St John's Gospel, they thought fit to add also the crooked nail of a horseshoe or a piece of wolf's skin, 'so far had they wandered into the ways of error in making these arms the strength of their healths'. And with childlike naivety, Psalm 8 was recited three times a day for three days as a cure for thrush, simply because there appeared in it the phrase, 'out of the mouths of babes and sucklings'.

Yet in those days the times were innocent, for where today could one find such an advertisement as this one:

'SMALL BAGGS to hang about Children's necks, which are excellent both for the *prevention* and *cure* of the Rickets, and to ease children in breeding of Teeth, are prepared by Mr. Edmund Buckworth, and constantly to be had at Mr. Philip Clark's, Keeper of the Library in the Fleet, and nowhere else, at 5 shillings a bagge.'

The Intelligencer, 16 Oct., 1664

SYMPATHETIC MAGIC

Time was not an inevitable aid to maturity of thought and growth away from foolish beliefs. Even up to the mid-nineteenth century people were known to remove portions of clay from the grave of a priest in order to make of it broth for the sick. Or else for toothache, they might remove the tooth of a corpse and, having placed it in a bag, hang it round the neck of the sufferer.

There were also the superstitious beliefs surrounding human hair. In most parts of the world, there was supposed a magical connection existing between a shorn lock of hair and the person to whom it had belonged. In India, as in ancient Greece, in cases of severe illness, hair was sometimes cut from the head and offered to the deity. In England it was at one time believed that if a person's hair burned brightly when thrown into a fire it was a sign of longevity; whereas if it smouldered slowly it was thought to be an omen of imminent death. In parts of Ireland it was believed that human hair should never be burnt, but always buried, since at the resurrection of the owner he would come back and seek his own hair.

The converse notion prevailed in Europe, demanding that the only proper disposal for cropped hair was consignment to the fire. Another fate to beware of in parts of Europe was the possession of one's locks by a witch, since that simple accident would subject their owner to sorcery. It was also as well to see that no bird ever wove strands of one's hair into its nest, for to do so would strike the unfortunate loser first with headaches and later with baldness. Finally, that lighthearted quip 'A hair of the dog,' that we quote as we offer a hang-over sufferer another drink, derives from the notion people once held that the cure for a dog-bite was quite literally the possession of some hairs from that same dog.

The practice of using dolls in the curing of disease was a form of witchcraft found almost universally. Among the Dyaks of Borneo, for instance, a small puppet shaped from boiled rice was fastened by the magician to the house of the patient. The sickness, it was believed, would pass to the doll, and after a time, when the doll was removed, the sickness likewise would also disappear.

In Samuel Pepys's day, feathers were reckoned an efficacious remedy. 'Pull off the feathers from the tail of living cocks,' wrote the great diarist, 'or even hens, pigeons or chickens; and holding their bills, press them hard to the botch or swelling and so keep them at that part till they die. By this means the poison will surely be drawn out.'

There may have been some fundamental healing property peculiar to the species, for a further account, reminiscent of the above, may be found in David Douglas' *Rhind Lectures* of 1876 where he cites the burial of a live cock for the cure of epilepsy. 'It is a sacrifice deliberately and consciously offered in order to propitiate a supernatural power, and effect the expulsion of the demon who is thought to have possession of the unfortunate epileptic. The ceremonies which attend the sacrifice leave little doubt as to its origin, or as to its past and present significance. It is nearly always gone about in a secret and solemn manner, in such a way as will best tend to secure its important object. A special superhuman agency, who is not the God of Christians, is acknowledged and appealed to, and an effort is made to avert his malevolence . . . It would be a great mistake to suppose that the persons referred to are the grossly ignorant, and a still greater mistake to suppose that they are the irreligious. On the contrary, they are often church-attending, sacrament-observing and tolerably well educated people;— people, too, who necessarily participate in all the advantages of the advanced civilisation of their country.'

THE ROYAL TOUCH

The function of the monarch is varied, and touches upon both state and church. In Stuart times the royal hand was expected not only to authorise translation of the scriptures, to sign the death warrant of a subject, but also to stretch forth that hand in healing of his subjects. Speaking of King James, Shakespeare in *Macbeth* showed Malcolm as saying, before the King's palace in England:

'A most miraculous work in this good king,
Which often since my here-remain in England
I have seen him do. How he solicits Heaven
Himself best knows: but strangely visited people,
All swoln and ulcerous, pitiful to the eye,
The mere despair of surgery he cures
Put on with holy prayers.'

Macbeth. IV.3

Hundreds were touched for scrofula. The king crossed the sores with a coin, known as an angel noble, which was hung around the sufferer's neck. The pressing sick became tiresome, however, and the king (so wearied, it seems, of his people's incessant clamour) decreed it necessary to publish the following advertisement:

'WHITEHALL, May 14, 1664. His Sacred Majesty, having declared it to be his Royal will and purpose to continue the healing of his people for the Evil during the Month of May, and then to give over till Michaelmas next, I am commanded to give notice thereof, that the people may not come to Town in the Interim and lose their labour.'

Public Intelligencer, 1664

One of the most commonly accepted natural cures relates to blindness; and as in the gospels Jesus the carpenter from Nazareth used spittle as a healing anointing, so this has been used down the generations since; (there are exceptions obviously, the healing of Tobit's sight by fish-gall to mention but one; but in the main, spittle was the usual substance for healing;) and there are diverse instances of it. Pliny recorded that, among the ancient peoples, the spittle of a woman fasting after her newly delivered first-born was a certain cure for bloodshot eyes. Captain Cook, during his voyage to the north-west coast of America, was called upon to heal an elderly man of blindness and, holding his breath and spitting on his eyelids, effected the cure.

A remarkable incident of this kind can be attested by the author: a young District Commissioner in East Africa who had mysteriously lost the sight of one eye and had been given no hope by an eminent ocular specialist, went finally in desperation to a local witch-doctor. Although reluctant and suspicious at first, the old healer agreed to help him. Grasping his head between her knees, she proceeded to lick his affected eye continuously until at last she produced the offending body, a grub.

Common sense explains this with facility, in the same way as it rationalises the application of saliva to insect bites. Yet there remains nonetheless an element of the supernatural in spittle. Why, for instance, do people in country areas still spit on money received in a business deal? Or for luck when they see a white horse? Why do some modern cricketers anoint the ball with spittle before they bowl each ball? Why used the priests of the Mandingoes, an African tribe, to spit three times into the face of a child when giving it a name? And what was the reason for the custom, in time past, of spitting into the grave as part of the funeral ceremony?

Then there is the enigma of the sneeze; believed to possess influence over the soul of a man and to have power to blow it out of the body, it became regarded as a potential killer, and the perfunctory lipservice, 'Bless you', that we pray today when someone sneezes reverts partly to that belief, but also to the time of Pope Gregory, (590–604) when a fatal epidemic raged whose confirmatory symptom was a sneeze. Thus in India, Africa and North America, where sneezing was an omen not of physical calamity but of the presence of evil spirits, it still called for the protective prayer of blessing.

PREDICTIONS OF DEATH

Death is regarded as man's last known enemy—paradoxically because it is itself unknown—and it is this mystery, this finality, which so baffles and frightens man. The physical act of dying, also, is fraught with fearful apprehension, both to the subject and those who will survive him. There is pain in the sharp break of familiar ties, and there is horror at the decomposition of the body. Death, it would seem, is an end. Yet, against all logic, it is found that even from earliest antiquity, man—in this instance, cave-man—has rejected this view of death, and far from regarding it as an end, has made the appropriate preparations to indicate quite clearly that he looked upon death as a period of transition. The physical body might die and decompose, yet there lived on some element of the human species, *homo sapiens*, which would require provision for the after-life.

So archaeology has unearthed urns of grain and caskets of gems from pyramids, sustenance and enrichment for their pharaoh occupant; while Hindu widows, performing the rite *Sati*, abolished in British India in 1829, threw themselves on the funeral pyres of their husbands to follow them faithfully into the life beyond death. Whether this is to say that our forebears believed in the soul of man as such is hard to say, but certainly they believed that part of man lived on after his physical body died. This immortal element took on various guises: in some eastern countries, for instance, it was regarded as being embodied in the raven. Most certainly in later times, and in the realms of fairy tales, the raven is an ominous foreboder of death. The ancient Jews would appear to have been curiously divided on the raven's significance; on the one hand regarding them as divine messengers like those which fed the prophet detested by King Ahab in I Kings 17.4, 6, while Genesis 8.7 records that the raven was given the responsibility of leaving the Ark first to scan the earth for vegetation or land after the flood. In the Pentateuch, on the other hand, ravens were classed as unclean and identified with such birds as the ostrich, the owl, the kite and the vulture (Lev. 11.14, 15, Deut. 14.14).

CHAPTER ELEVEN

Giving Up the Ghost

DEATH, THE last enemy, is feared by man on two counts: it is the final severance from a loved one; it is an irrevocable step into the unknown. So man made provision to meet these contingencies. Dreading death, he waited and watched for imminent signs of it; he made every provision possible for the well-being of the corpse when the time came; and he went to fastidious lengths to prevent the soul of the corpse remaining earthbound.

The chief portents of death besides the dreaded sneeze of the great plague were animals of various kinds and visions. Aids to speedier, easier death varied from antipathy for feather death-beds and the opening up of all doors to facilitate the soul's escape, to Christmas euthanasia, Christmas Eve being regarded as the only day on which one could die and escape purgatory. The superstitions surrounding the corpse after death included solicitude by mourners for the buried corpse, and alongside this commendable concern a quite indisputable solicitude for those left behind, with emphatic ritual consequently to insure that the soul of the corpse made good its departure and did not linger earth-bound molesting the lives of the bereaved.

There were also hardy practices to ensure that a corpse had really died; yet at heart all was done in good faith, and to ensure that the soul of the deceased was given every opportunity to reach the climes where it would achieve rest and peace.

Akin to this belief was that held in parts of Switzerland, which maintained that to find the raven's fellow, the crow, perching on a house-top in which lay a corpse was a sure indication that the soul of the late owner of that body was damned.

The hoot of an owl perched on the roof of a house was said to be a death-omen. Even to hear the cry of an owl at night was considered unlucky. To hear it in the daytime, however, was a sure omen of grave misfortune. In the Montgomeryshire village of Castle Caereinion, an owl hooting from one of the churchyard yew trees meant the death-knell to someone in the parish, and to catch sight of the way in which the bird was facing was to have an intimation of the location of the unfortunate house the angel of death planned to visit. This omen occurs in Chaucer:

> 'The jelous Swan, ayenst deth that singeth,
> The Oule eke, that of deth the bode bringeth.'
> *(Assembly of Foules)*

Just as ominous in Britain as the owl is the robin. In all parts robins are held in high esteem, probably due to a superstition once held that if a robin came upon a dead body it set about covering it with leaves, as the story of the Babes in the Wood bears witness. From this seems to have grown the notion that it is unlucky to kill or keep a robin:

> 'A Robin Red breast in a Cage,
> Puts all Heaven in a Rage.'
> (Blake, *Auguries of Innocence*)

Nevertheless, to have one fly into a house is to disrupt most severely the repose of the dwellers, for it is believed to be uncannily possessed of the premonition of death. Fitzpatrick writes in his *Life of Bishop Doyle*, 'Considering that the season was midsummer, and not winter, the visit of two robin redbreasts to the sick-room may be noticed as interesting. They remained fluttering round and sometimes perching on the uncurtained bed. The priests, struck by the novelty of the circumstance, made no effort to expel the little visitors, and the robins hung lovingly over the bishop's head until death released him.'

Comparable with this superstition is that which dreaded the discovery of a jackdaw or swallow in the fireplace, for this also was a token of death. Yet not all superstitious beliefs surrounding birds are of evil portent. Brazilian savages believed that only the souls of the courageous became transmuted into birds: those whose lives had been evil were banished for the after life into the forms of reptiles.

In nautical annals rats are conspicuously ominous when they

leave a ship. Away from the sea, it has been the mouse which heralded bad tidings. From as far afield as Russia and Devonshire it was believed that death was surely imminent when a mouse appeared for the first time in a house. A mouse running over a sick person was considered to be an infallible sign of death, as was a mouse squeaking behind a bed in which there was an invalid; and country people at one time had the fixed idea that a harvest-mouse was unable to cross in safety a path which had been used by men. Whenever they made the attempt, they were immediately struck dead. It is certainly true that one often finds these little rodents lying dead on the verge of a field footpath, having no external wound or apparent cause of death.

Random investigation will yield quite a considerable variety of creatures which are associated with death, from such oddities as a crowing hen, lice (one in one's linen for sickness, two for severer illness, and three for the ultimate dread of death), to the commonplace cat which possessed power to 'draw away the health of an infant', or even that of over-devoted adults, till the traditionally recognised and sinister figure of the dog baying at the full moon is reached. Dogs were quite commonly believed to have communication with the spirit world, and if the dog sat and howled by the door it was taken as a sure sign that someone in the family was about to sicken or die. An acquaintance of the author had the experience of entering a supposedly haunted room in a house with his two dogs and seeing both of them cower petrified against the walls as though excruciatingly aware of some supernatural presence there.

Equally sinister was the superstition surrounding the powers of perception that pigs possessed. In certain farming communities in Brittany and Western Ireland the belief prevailed that the pig sensed the impending death of the farmer and reacted by whining. The superstition was the more eerie since this signal was recognisable only by the victim himself.

In parts of France and Germany and in England, there prevailed in the Dark Ages the superstition that oxen were given the power of speech on Christmas Eve. There was, however, a great deterrent fear, which tempered the curiosity of those wanting to put this notion to the proof; for the belief was that the listeners never heard any good of themselves, and, worse, that such bovine utterances were predictions of sudden death.

Not unlike this superstition was the belief in the early nineteenth century of the peasantry of many Austrian villages that if between eleven o'clock and midnight on the Eve of St John a person washed in the water of three wells, he would be granted power to see in a vision all those who were to die in the following year.

A portent of death which was general years ago involved the passing of a funeral. 'He who meets one is certain to die unless he takes his headwear off, turns, and walks along with the coffin for a little way.' If the coffin was carried by bearers he had to lend a hand. Having done this and bowed to the mourners, he was then free to go on his way without fear of death.

It is still said in certain places in the north of England that funerals happen in threes; when one occurs two more will follow very rapidly. The same idea prevailed in Rome where the Sacred College of Cardinals was concerned, for it was said that cardinals always died in threes.

Many are the superstitions associated with warnings of death, and none more appropriate in a survey of religious superstitions than those given by church bells. Should the church clock strike during the hymn before the sermon or during the announcement of its text, this was taken to mean there would be a death in that parish before the week was out.

DEATH AIDS

The wish 'to die with your boots on' might be an echo of that curious notion, prevalent until the last century, that men could not die easy in a bed. Evidence can be found of peasant people from Bolton to Bangladesh, of whatever creed, taking the dying out of their beds and laying them down on the floor in order to facilitate the departure of their souls. In some parts of the world this superstition was confined to a fastidiousness about feather-beds only (especially those made from the feathers of pigeons or game fowl) and Russian peasants in particular had an antipathy for the use of pigeon feathers in mattresses as being sacrilegious, since the dove was an emblem of the Holy Spirit.

An extraordinary belief in Ireland, claiming that anyone dying on Christmas Eve was spared the rigours of purgatory, led to many an unfortunate body being precipitated over the brink prematurely by the deliberate action of his relatives or friends.

In *Guy Mannering* by Sir Walter Scott, we find an incident very similar to the belief prevailing in southern Spain, Germany and England, of opening the doors and windows of a house where there was a corpse to permit its soul free passage on its journey: '"He cannot pass away with that on his mind—it tethers him here:

> Heaven cannot abide it,
> Earth refuses to hide it.

I must open the door;" and, rising, she faced towards the door of the apartment, observing heedfully not to turn back her head, and, withdrawing a bolt or two, she lifted the latch saying,

> "Open lock—end strife,
> Come death, and pass life."'

An explanatory note on this passage by the correspondent of *Blackwood's Magazine* read:

'The popular idea, that the protracted struggle between life and death is painfully prolonged by keeping the door of the apartment shut, was received as certain by the superstitious eld of Scotland. But neither was it to be thrown wide open. To leave the door ajar, was the plan adopted by the old crones who understood the mysteries of death-beds and lyke-wakes. In that case, there was room for the imprisoned spirit to escape; and yet an obstacle, we have been assured, was offered to the entrance of any frightful form which might otherwise intrude itself. The threshold of a habitation was in some sort a sacred limit, and the subject of much superstition.'

In the same vein of thought is an old Dutch superstition: it was once the practice in parts of Holland, when a child was dying, to surround it with curtains so that the parents should not gaze upon it, for the notion was that the child would not die but linger on until the parents were prepared to give it up.

DEATH BED RITUAL

Death-bed ritual seems to have evolved through fear of pollution, both from the ghost of the dead person and from contact with death itself. Pausanias, the traitor-king of Sparta, when he fled for sanctuary to the temple of Athene, was blockaded and starved almost to death, since no one dared touch him. Only at the very last moment, when he was on the point of death, was he dragged out just in time to die outside the temple, thus avoiding polluting it.

Among the Jews at Gibraltar there was a strange superstition that, when death occurred in a house, all the water in any vessel had to be poured away; the belief being that the angel of death might have washed his sword in it. And in the Numbers 19.15, the Levitical Law decreed that any uncovered vessel standing in the tent where anyone had died was unclean for seven days.

Among gypsies, it was the practice to burn the clothes of their dead, not so much because they were afraid of catching any infection from them, but because they stoutly believed that to wear them would shorten the days of the living. In another superstition, fire was employed as a symbol of mourning and identification with the corpse; thus the fire in the hearth —the soul of the household—was extinguished. (If it were kept alight this was explicitly done as protection against evil spirits.) Fires were not the only things to die with a corpse. It is still customary to hear of a clock ceasing to tick with the death of an occupant of the house.

For those relatives left, ceremonial rites were in order before burial; thus lamentation and dirges began at the moment of death and the corpse was watched over until the funeral. Ceremonial eating and drinking in the presence of the dead was not uncommon in European countries. It is said that in Upper Bavaria the dough used for making the 'corpse cakes' was set to rise on the dead body itself. The superstition was that the cakes then contained the riches and advantages of the deceased, and that in this way the living strength of the departed passed over into the relatives who consumed the cakes and was thus retained within the clan.

Once death had taken place in a house and the attendant

rites were complete, everything possible was then done to prevent the spirit of the deceased being hindered in its journey. Thus, besides opening doors, some folk covered every looking-glass in the house also. If this were not done between the corpse's death and funeral, it was quite possible that it might be tempted to linger on in its old habitation, and for the living to look into a mirror in the death-chamber was surely to see the corpse looking into it as well over your shoulder.

When death occurred in the early days of the Roman empire, all those standing round the death-bed raised a cry. This was done for two reasons: in the first place with the hope of re-calling the corpse to life; or, should he not revive, it served to confirm death. Very similar was the Irish custom of howling over the dead, since the corpse was not assumed really dead until the wailing failed to restore the spirit to the body.

A curious death superstition was established amongst bee-keepers. In some parts, on the death of the owner of hives or bees, a scarf or black crêpe was attached to each bee-hive; and an offering of pounded funeral biscuit, soaked in wine, was placed at its entrance. Yet another superstition was that of inviting bees to funerals. When a death occurred, a person was appointed to call the neighbours to the funeral, and he de-livered the invitations thus: 'You are invited to the funeral of Mr X. which is to take place at such an hour, on such a day; and there will be dinner on table at . . . . 'clock.' It was believed that, unless the same invitation was extended to the bees in their hives, they would die. A derivative of this practice was found in Cornwall, where a death was reported to the cattle, while in other countries it was trees that had to be specifically instructed of a man's recent passing.

SPIRITS OF THE DEAD

Not only were souls facilitated in their journeys away from the earthly sphere; in many parts of the world strict precautions were taken to prevent the spirit of the dead body returning. In some areas, before the body was removed from its past home, it was dismembered; or the limbs were tied together, and in-variably the corpse was removed from the house feet first to prevent the dead man seeing his way back. This practice of confusing and puzzling the corpse was shared by the civilised nations of Europe with the savages of Mabuiog in Torres Straits.

It is recorded that, when David Hume, the historian, philosopher and sceptic, died and was buried, 'the piety or caution of his friends made them watch the grave for some eight nights after the burial. The vigil began at eight o'clock, when a pistol was fired, and candles in a lanthorn were placed on the grave and tended from time to time, for some violation was feared since a wild legend of Satanic agency had flashed on the instant throughout all the town.'

In the reign of Hammurabi (1728–1686 BC), funeral rites in Babylon (where the corpse was buried in a clay 'bath tub' coffin) included the dutiful ministrations of surviving relatives in order that the libations and offerings made by them might keep the corpse undisturbed and at peace. The retribution for neglect of these duties was certain and dreadful: the corpse would not hesitate to rise from its grave and demand its rights. (The deliberate removal of the bones from the tomb forced the spirit to wander homeless, earthbound and bent on mischief.) All sorts of calamities were attributed to these wandering ghosts, such as the death of a person who drowned, the mother who died in childbirth, or the death of a virgin or bachelor.

Action taken by American Indians to protect them from the angry ghosts of their victims consisted in running through their villages beating with sticks the walls and roofs of their dwellings. Frazer recorded the statement of a traveller who reported that, 'on approaching in the night a village of Ottawas, I found all the inhabitants in confusion: they were all busily engaged in raising noises of the loudest and most inharmonious kind. Upon inquiry, I found that a battle had been lately fought between the Ottawas and the Kickapoos, and that the object of all this noise was to prevent the ghosts of the departed combatants from entering the village.'

The belief that widows were haunted by the spirits of their late husbands was at one time widespread. In the preface to one of his novels, Sir Walter Scott tells of a pirate who was ultimately caught and hanged for his crimes. He was engaged to an Orkney girl, and she went up to London to see him before his death. Arriving too late, she had the courage to request a sight of her lover's dead body; and then, touching the hand of the corpse, she formally resumed the troth-plight which she had bestowed. 'Without going through the ceremony,' says Sir Walter, 'she could not, according to the superstition of the country, have escaped a visit from the ghost of her departed lover, in the event of her bestowing upon any living suitor the faith which she had plighted to the dead.'

Among the Arunta of central Australia, when a man died his wives would smear their hair, faces, and breasts with clay, and preserve silence for a period of mourning which lasted anything up to twelve months.

The Yoruba widow in south-western Nigeria mourned her husband for three months, during which time she was not to plait her hair, take a bath, or remove the clothes she was wearing when her husband died. She was confined to her hut during the daytime and allowed to go out only very rarely after dark.

In Papua the widow was compelled to lie close to her husband's grave during her period of mourning which lasted for three months. This was made possible by covering the grave with a mat and putting a roof of branches over it. In Western countries funeral superstitions took a somewhat different turn. More rooted in Christian foundations, the superstitious practices revolved around the religious ceremonies attaching to burial. So folklore tells that in the seventeenth century, after the funeral sermon was preached, wine, wafers, gloves and rosemary were distributed among the mourners. Also in European countries a female relative of the deceased would hand over coffin-loaves of bread and some cheese stuck with coins as the corpse was carried out of the house. The recipients of the bread and cheese were thus believed to take away the sins of the deceased, for which reason these people earned the name 'sin-eaters'. Certainly the term was well known in Wales during the nineteenth century. They were then given, in the same manner, a drink from a common cup. This was immediately followed by the saying of the Lord's prayer, after which the cortège proceeded slowly to the graveyard stopping at every crossroads between the house of the deceased and the grave for further recitals of the Lord's prayer. All that now remains of this superstition is the festive side of interments. Wakes are an important feature in Ireland, and no less in other parts of Britain, and in the United States. In South Wales corpses are chattily 'buried with ham', the phrase indicating the hearty meal the mourners enjoy after the deceased has been duly interred. That this practice could be connected with the more sinister or quaint appendices of death beliefs is not really likely, however, it being more in the keeping of a parting meal in honour of the deceased.

PARTING PROPHECY

A belief sprang up from Roman and Greek times which claimed that the dying, particularly those who had led holy lives, were endowed for a brief time before death, with the power of prophecy; this was claimed of Aristotle, for instance, and thus Homer in the *Iliad* made the dying Hector foretell the end of Achilles, 'when Apollo and Paris shall subdue thee at the gates of Troy'. And not only the dying prophesied. Some folk claimed to have heard predictions emanate from actual corpses. If the corpse stiffened shortly after death, all was taken as normal; but if the limbs remained flexible, some-one in the family was surely soon to follow. Similarly, if the eyes of a corpse were difficult to close, it was said that 'they were looking after a follower'.

A superstition, dangerous to the innocent, prevailed for a long time in many European countries. It maintained that a murdered person would bleed, even when dead, at the touch of the murderer. It was even thought that the presence of the murderer (even though he did not come into contact with the corpse) would have the same effect. So in Germany it became customary that the suspect was bidden to put two fingers on the face of the deceased, next on the wound which caused death, and afterwards on the navel. This he had to do in the presence of a priest who adjured him to appeal to heaven. The origin of this story may well have some connection with the Genesis story of the world's first murder, of Abel by Cain, when God challenged the elder brother Cain with the stern caution, 'the voice of your brother's blood cries out to me from the very ground' (Gen. 4).

According to Mark Twain in his book *Huckleberry Finn* an American superstition maintains that a drowned man will float face downwards in the water, while a woman who has died by drowning floats face uppermost.

Associated deviously with the resurrection of Jesus Christ on

the third day, another superstition claims that in three days
the expression of a corpse becomes placid. Thus, in spite of
the threats of owls, ravens, dogs or church bells; despite the
indignities of being put out of bed to die on the floor or the
inhumanity of being despatched to eternity before the proper
time, and in peril of being left earthbound by negligent relatives,
or banished by dismembering for fear of biding—finally, nevertheless, endowed with powers of prophecy and detection, the
soul of the deceased eventually found repose and peace.

CHAPTER TWELVE

Disposal with Dignity

HAND IN HAND with the pathological fear man has for earthbound spirits goes his equally great concern for the soul of the departed and its well-being in the after-life. Shakespeare has matchlessly epitomised our awe for spirits, and the exploiters of macabre sensation imbue most of us at one time or another with the icy morbidity supposed to pervade burial-places, disturbing men's calm with fear of malevolence or mischief. It may well have been this fundamental human fear which compelled ancient peoples to take such elaborate steps to ensure the safe repose of the dead. The nations of the Near and Far East, the Indians of North America, and the European peoples all have traditions practical, quaint, even droll, for accommodating the dead in their after-life.

It was comparable expediencies which determined methods or place of burial: cremation, burial (under ground, above ground, at sea), embalming, cannibalism, all stemmed from solicitude or common sense, the main purpose for the choice being either the safety of the departed soul, or its successful arrival at its final destination.

RESTLESS SPIRITS

For all our cut-and-dried talk of souls going either to heaven or to hell after death, there flourishes an astonishingly ubiquitous apprehension of burial-places, particularly at night. Shakespeare summed up the fear in his play *Hamlet*, with the utterance,

''Tis now the very witching time of night,
When churchyards yawn and hell itself breathes out
Contagion to this world:'

(Hamlet, III. ii)

There is something doubly eerie in the implication of that word 'yawn'. Generally associated with comforting sleep, here it implies the sinister imminence of the dead rising from their graves, 'in churchyard paths to glide', until dawn, described by Puck as,

'And yonder shines Aurora's harbinger;
At whose approach, ghosts, wandering here and there,
Troop home to churchyards:'

(*A Midsummer Night's Dream*, III.ii)

Nor is it singularly the burial-place which creates this ghoulish atmosphere. The darkness of night is a redoubtable partner in the drama. It is at night that spirits wander most often, and during the hours of darkness they are most feared. The classical story of Israel wrestling all night with the angel of God substantiates this whole belief grounded in man from earliest history; they were, by open admission, supernatural beings, and one of their preferred habitats was water, and their time was undoubtedly night.

This is not to say, however, that these restless spirits of the dead wandered only in darkness. The author knew a woman who was at one time a children's nurse. Taking her two charges to an afternoon tea-party, she commented on the shy persistence of a small boy amongst the children playing games and drew someone's attention to him. 'The child over there with red socks,' she indicated. 'Oh Red Socks,' was the rejoinder; 'he turns up now and again; used to live in this manor house till he died in the fire here.'

For the most part, however, the souls of the departed who cannot find an eternal niche, but who wander earthbound, are nocturnal beings, and are regarded as much with pity as with fear. Men are concerned that they seem unable to reach their eternal resting-place, and it was this concern which contributed to the meticulous and thoughtful preparations of the living for the dead. The most lavish and classical examples of this are found in the splendidly furnished and provisioned tombs of the Egyptian Pharaohs and ancient Chinese, and there is evidence that even Neolithic man believed in a future state beyond death. Thus he, also, buried gifts with the corpse: personal ornaments, beads of amber, bracelets and shells, with the intention of accommodating the corpse as fittingly as possible for the continuation of his life in the next world. Such quirks still exist indeed. Not so long ago a maiden lady was buried in Cheshire with the accompaniment in her coffin of her greatly treasured reproduction picture of 'The Laughing Cavalier'. Absurd, perhaps, one might think at first, and yet no more far-fetched than the stocks of grain and drinking-vessels left in ancient tombs for the sustenance of the deceased.

Comfort featured largely also. In Sweden at one time it was the custom to bury with a man his pipe, tobacco-pouch, a little money and some lights. It was not unusual for attempts to be made to warm the ghost, as was the case with the Tarahumares of Mexico, who buried their dead in caves, lighting a fire at or on the grave the first night after burial. The Seminoles of Florida made a fire at each end of the grave and kept it burning for three days and nights to protect the corpse from evil spirits. The Hupa and the Yorok Indians in California believed the fire was necessary to light the spirit of the departed on its journey to the spirit world.

Footwear was an important item as well. In Russia and California it has been found that the corpse was shod with a pair of new shoes in order that he might be adequately prepared for his long journey. A curious variant of this practice came to light in Ireland where the deceased were buried with some footwear in order to protect their feet when they carried out their duties of watering those buried in the churchyard. This practice may have derived from the superstitious belief that, should two funerals take place in the same grave-yard on the same day, the last corpse buried was obliged to carry water to allay the thirst of all those others buried there previously! This naturally caused trouble from time to time, and the skirmishes which broke out between rival burial parties became known as the Battles of the Derrins. One such fight was described by T. P. Le Fanu:

'Two funerals were approaching Abington churchyard in opposite directions, one from Murroe the other from Barrington's Bridge. The former was nearing the churchyard gate; on perceiving this the people in the other funeral took a short cut by running across a field, carrying the coffin with them, which they succeeded in throwing over the wall of the churchyard before the others were able to get in by the gate.' The result of this chicanery was what was to be expected, a 'battle of the Derrin's to vindicate the honour of the slighted corpse.

A less militant method of pacifying departed souls was to cut a turf four inches square from the deceased person's grave and leave the turf under or on the altar of the church for four days. There is an instance of this very act in *The Warrington Guardian* for 26 November 1881, recording the request of a woman of the vicar of Lower Gornal, Staffordshire, for a four-inch square turf from the grave of a man who apparently was restless because of a guilty conscience. The turf, the account continued, was put on the Communion table in order to dispel the ghost. A less pleasant method of obtaining the same effect is recorded in the *Journal of American Folklore* when a member of the Omaha Indians of North America was killed by lightning: it was the practice to bury the body on the very spot where death occurred, face downwards, with the soles of the feet previously slit as a precaution against haunting.

In order to afford the dead every possible advantage on the final day of judgement when all souls would be called forth, it was the practice to lay a corpse to rest with its face pointing to the east. In origin this was a relic of sun-worship, continued and adapted by the early Christians who believed that the Last Judgement would come from the east. There was, too, the practice of burying the corpse face downwards, since some people believed that the world would turn over on the Last Day and, buried thus, the person would be assured of the advantage of facing the right side up. It was also believed by some superstitious people that if a corpse was buried face downwards, then any evil spirit haunting the grave would be confused and lose its direction.

There is a curious incident recorded by a cleric in Northumberland in 1860 related to the notion that to bury a stillborn child in an open grave would ensure direct passage to heaven for the next adult buried in that grave.

'When I was curate at Newburn in Northumberland,' wrote Canon Humble in 1860, 'the custom was to bring the coffin of an unbaptised babe with that of a full grown person. The child's coffin was always laid on the other coffin towards the feet, and so rested while the service was said. There was generally a receptacle for it in the grave towards the feet, made by widening the grave at that point.'

The graves of stillborn children have ever been surrounded by superstitious practices. In some parts, as stated above, they were regarded as most beneficial; but not everywhere. It was also known for such graves to be carefully avoided because it was believed that to step on the grave of a stillborn child might develop in the offender 'grave-merels' or 'grave-scab', a disease which consisted not only in a burning skin but also in trembling limbs and restricted breathing.

> 'To see a man tread over graves,
>   I hold it no good mark;
> 'Tis wicked in the sun and moon,
>   And bad luck in the dark!'
>
> (Coleridge, *The Three Graves*)

OUT IN THE COLD

Baring Gould makes mention of the fact that it was the custom in ancient times to bury a dog or a boar alive under the cornerstone of a church, in order that its ghost might haunt the churchyard and drive off any who would profane it, such as witches or warlocks. Should such evil influences pervade a burial place, it was inevitably the north side of it. Though the whole churchyard was hallowed, and equally consecrated, that quarter was ill favoured and reserved for the graves of suicides, unbaptised persons and stillborn infants.

In order to dispel this heretical notion, the priest of a parish in England stipulated that his body be buried on the north side of his church. This was duly done—an action which persuaded his rich and well-to-do parishioners to follow his example at their death. The poor, however, stoutly held to the old superstition and, convinced that it was an uncanny place, if not the haunt of evil spirits, elected to continue their preference to be interred elsewhere.

That great pastor and character R. S. Hawker, Vicar of Morwenstow, sums up the notion thus: 'The North side is included in the same consecration with rest of the ground. All within the boundary, and the boundary itself, is alike hallowed in sacred and secular law. It is because of the doctrine of the

Regions, which has descended unbrokenly in the Church, that an evil repute rests on the northern parts. The East, from whence the Son of Man came, and who will come again from the Orient to judgement, was, and is, his own special realm. The dead lie with their feet and faces turned eastwardly, ready to stand up before the approaching Judge. The West was called the Galilee, the region of the people. The South, home of the noonday, was the typical domain of heavenly things. But the North, the ill-omen North, was the peculiar haunt of evil spirits and the dark powers of the air. Satan's door stood in the North wall, opposite the font, and was duly opened at the exorcism in baptism for the egress of the fiend. When our Lord lay in the sepulchre, it was with feet towards the East, so that his right hand gave benediction to the South and his left hand reproached the repelled North. When the evil spirits were cast out by the voice of the Messiah, they fled ever more northward. The god of the North was Baalzephon. They say that at the North Pole there stands the awful gate, which none may approach and live, and which leads to the central depths of penal life.'

Random research, nonetheless, still presents persistence and varied pedantries where people's preferences were concerned as to the better and less favourable burial-spots in churchyards. 'The left side of Christ, sir; we don't like to be counted among the goats.' Such is the plebeian interpretation of the parable in St Matthew's gospel on the sheep and the goats, where the Son of Man shall set the sheep on his right hand but the goats on the left.

And in the same way north-side burials were improper as being reserved for suicides and the like:

> ''Tis said that some have died for love:
> And here and there a churchyard grave is found
> In the cold North's unhallowed ground,
> Because the wretched man himself had slain,
> His love was such a grievous pain.'
>
> (Wordsworth)

Some suicides were buried in quicklime at the four cross-roads at midnight. And in some parts of the country when the corpse of a suicide was buried, the coffin was turned upside down, and a spear was driven through the body to pin it to the ground in order to prevent the dead person from 'walking'.

There is a macabre account in William Brockie's *Legends and Superstitions of the County of Durham*, 1886, of such a burial at a crossroads, where the local village lads used to amuse themselves standing upon the stake which marked the grave of the unfortunate baker buried beneath.

In 1823, however, an Act was given the royal assent 'to alter and amend the law relating to the interment of the remains of a person found *Felo de se*,' (a self-murderer). The Act, 4 George IV, c.52, directed that the interment of the bodies of suicides be in the churchyard or other burial ground within twenty-four hours of the coroner's inquest, but still at night, between the hours of nine and midnight, and they were excluded from Christian burial.

WAYS AND MEANS

The methods of disposal of the dead in various parts of the world depended in no little measure on the particular belief regarding the state of the soul after life. The Place of the Dead was believed to be under ground as was Sheol in the belief of the ancient Hebrews. If it were beyond the sea, however, then the body was placed in a canoe or ship. There is evidence that in Polynesia preservation of the dead above ground was practised, especially of the chiefs whose souls were believed to live in the sky.

Even in the Stone Age, the body was burnt, most probably to prevent a return of the dangerous ghost. Around 1300 BC, however, cremation became the general practice over the greater part of central and northern Europe, in Italy and Britain, but it did not entirely oust the older rite of inhumation. At this time the consuming of the body with fire seems to have been associated with a new belief that the soul or spirit continued after death in a remote dwelling in the sky to which it ascended with the smoke of the funeral pyre.

In Britain these artificial mounds can still be seen, usually on elevated land. These *tumuli* or *barrows* are the ancient burial-grounds of the early inhabitants of our island. Such places are surrounded by superstition. Some believe even now that if you run around a barrow nine times, then lie on the ground with your ear pressed to it, you will hear fairies singing and dancing inside. Certainly our forefathers believed that fairies inhabited the depths of these sacred places and that, as long as the *tumuli* remained undisturbed the power of the fairies mended broken bones and even ploughshares. But should the burial places be disturbed by any avaricious person looking for treasure, then the burning wrath of the little folk would assuredly be aroused.

In the days of sailing vessels, when wrecks were not uncommon off the British coast, it was believed that if a drowning man was rescued, the sea would in time take the life of the rescuer since it would not be cheated of its prey. Burial below the high-tide mark for a corpse washed up by the sea was therefore common for this reason. An Act of Parliament of 1808, however, provided for the decent burial of such corpses in churchyards, and at the expense of the parish. An interesting instance of this may be seen in the small and ancient Welsh churchyard of Pembrey where the niece of Napoleon is buried after being lost at sea off that coast.

Something has been said of the provision made to safeguard the quiet repose of the deceased's soul, and consequently the ease of the living; there was, however, another dread our forefathers had to contend with—ghouls. These were likely to attack the corpse. Consequently, very careful ministrations were necessary for its protection; thus the sign of the cross was placed on tombs, and the Sacrament was sometimes buried with the dead. Similarly, burial in churches, and preferably in the chancel before the altar, was believed to give special protection to the dead. The Rev. Thomas Lewis in 1721 asked if people could believe 'that the Carcasses of the Dead which polluted the Temples before, could give them Consecration which would invert the Nature of Things?' He claimed that 'the BURYING of the DEAD in CHURCHES and CHURCHYARDS may be prejudicial to the LIVING', and maintained that the 'Doctrine of the MASS was invented . . . to compleat the Cheat, that is, to bring SUPERSTITION to its Zenith, and perfect the Design of enriching the Coffers of the POPE and CLERGY . . . And therefore, those places where, or near to which the Mass was celebrated, were preferable to all other, and no Cost was to be spared for the obtaining so great a Benefit.' (*Seasonable Considerations on the Indecent and Dangerous Custom of*

BURYING in Churches and Churchyards, with remarkable OBSERVATIONS historical and philosophical. Proving that the Custom is not only contrary to the Practice of the Ancients, but fatal, in case of INFECTION' Rev. Thomas Lewis, 1721.)

To be the first corpse buried in a new graveyard was to be made the devil's possession, it was widely supposed. In Germany and Scandinavia, however, there was an antidote for this; by burying a dog or pig in the churchyard before any Christian burial took place, the curse was removed, the ground once more hallowed, and the interred rendered invulnerable.

SPIRIT PROTECTION

In an overgrown garden in Uganda stands a small white marble cross marking the Christian burial-place of a European child; yet powerful though the challenge and support of the Christian faith may be, the spontaneous reactions of a Ugandan, only recently converted from pagan traditions, coming upon that cross unexpectedly was one not of assurance but of terror. Indeed graveyards of Christian tombstones arouse in the hearts of long-civilised European peoples, the same irrational spontaneous fear of the spirits of the dead. Sophistication or instilled Christian belief has little bearing upon deep-seated superstitious maintenance. It was this which led to the urgency of promoting satisfactory funeral arrangements in order that the spirits might be placated. Thus to ensure safety from those who might be malevolent, and to honour those who were benevolent, the burial of food, gifts and other tokens was employed. In some primitive tribes the measures taken were cannibalistic. The superstitious belief was that to eat your dead relatives would guarantee the safe keeping of their spirits within the family.

Two contradictory superstitions concerning burial revolve around the actual burial-place—the house of the corpse. An obscure people of South America, believing the deceased to continue some mysterious form of life after death left the dead man in a hut which necessitated provision of a door in order that he should not suffer the cruelty of imprisonment. Baganda kings, on the other hand, were buried within the royal hut, which was then razed to the ground upon them.

Other variations of this superstitious practice are found

scattered as far across the globe as North Africa and America. There was, therefore, the time when the Comanche Indians of Texas killed a favourite wife at her husband's funeral, and Zulus some of the chief's slaves when the latter died, in order that the comforts of the deceased should continue to be properly attended to in eternity, as they had been on earth.

The Muslims developed this notion to erotic sublimity; according to the Koran, every believer would have awaiting him in paradise seventy-two dark-eyed maidens, who were imbued not only with eternal youth but also renewable virginity. And not only that; union with these exquisite creatures was fruitful or the reverse, simply according to the wishes of the believer.

There are other variants of the superstition which demanded some kind of aperture for the deceased's movement. The Delaware Indian made a hole in the head of the coffin in order that the soul of the corpse could have free passage to and fro while searching for some suitable spot for its final resting-place.

In Egypt mummies and pyramids were the result of efforts made by the early Egyptians to preserve their dead from interference and corruption. The body was mummified because it was believed that even in the afterlife it would still be needed, and that if it decayed or was in some way destroyed, a second and more fatal death would occur. So the pyramid was piled over the tomb chamber in an attempt to conceal the exact location of the body and thus prevent the destruction which would bring about its second death.

As for the coffins themselves, although during the reign of Hammurabi they were made of clay, nothing less than pure gold was considered good enough to form the actual receptacle for the dead Tutankhamen's remains, and the innermost coffin was more than six feet long and made of solid gold a quarter of an inch thick.

JOURNEY TO THE UNKNOWN

There used to be an old Welsh superstition which told of a mysterious light that flickered along the path which the next funeral would take. This corpse-candle was believed sometimes to be accompanied by a skull, or at other times, by an apparition of the person who was about to die. It moved into the church-yard and finally hovered about the place where the grave would be. An old tradition maintains that this strange phenomenon was granted to the Diocese of St David 'in answer to the Saint's prayer that his people might have evidence of the unseen world.'

For centuries the extinguished torch has been used as the symbol of death, and the superstitious mind has ever associated the soul with a flame. The old practice of burying a candle with a corpse to light the way for the soul to the next world was at one time common, but the custom has its origin in the practice of human sacrifice, the candle being a substitute for an ex-tinguished life. Human sacrifice was not uncommon in pagan times on the occasion of the burial of an important person. Thus Herodotus recorded that at the death of a king of Scythia one of his concubines, his cup-bearer, cook, groom, lackey and messenger were all sacrificed on his grave.

It is an interesting paradox that, although they developed a faith in monotheism very early and thus showed an advanced level of maturity in matters religious, the Hebrews offer very little conclusive evidence of their belief in life after death from Old Testament sources. On the other hand it is almost un-challenged fact that primitive man with his naïve, polytheistic beliefs had a positive belief in an after-life and took for granted the fact that, at death, a soul had to make a journey from this world to some other. A common idea in this conception was the notion that a sea, a lake, or a river was crossed. The Romans believed the shades were ferried across by Charon; faithful Mohammedans journeyed to their paradise over a bridge formed of a single hair; some tribes in Malaya thought that a fallen tree-trunk placed across a boiling lake gave access to the abode of the dead known to them as the Island of Fruits; John Bunyan's Pilgrim forded the River of Death.

Men also made provision for the journey of the soul. We have seen how the Eastern peoples provided food and precious stones for sustenance and comfort. They also took account of the fact that the journey would be unfamiliar and therefore undertook measures to facilitate its accomplishment. So it is known that the Eskimos of Greenland buried a dog's head with a child in the belief that canine experience would guide inexperienced youth, and the Greeks had the custom of providing their dead with the fare demanded by Charon for the ferry of the Styx.

St Augustine denounced this practice soundly, as 'a pernicious error' putting provision on the tombs of the dead, 'as if their souls came forth from the body and wanted food.' Nonetheless, in spite of teaching by so authoritative a man, such superstitious notions still persisted, and it is recorded that as late as the seventeenth century a woman stipulated that her coffin was to have a lock and key, the latter to be left clasped in her dead hand so that she might release herself from the tomb at leisure.

COLOURFUL END

Colour has played a significant part in mourning rituals. The Syrians and Armenians wear light blue, symbolic of the hope of heaven. White is the mourning colour in China, whereas black with its undertones of gloom and sense of loss is used in America and Europe. The South Sea Islanders wear a mixture of black and white, while the Persian mourning colour is that of withered leaves. In Burma and many other Far Eastern countries, as well as amongst the people of Maya in Central America, yellow is the colour of mourning and of the land of the dead. (Comparable with this is the custom in some parts of putting yellow flowers on graves on All Souls' Day.) And for Royalty and the dignitaries of the Church, the traditional mourning hue has always been purple or violet.

It was also a sign of grief to cover the head. From the Israelites to the Greeks and Romans, on to the Anglo Saxons and up to the present day, this is observed, the current covering being a black veil.

The reasons for these diverse preferences are as different as the preferences themselves, though the fundamental consideration is respect for the dead, whether from the point of view of loss by the bereaved or of tribute to the deceased. On the surface they are vain superstitious notions—like every other religious superstition—all of religion that remains when practising belief is gone. Yet they nonetheless remain as symbols— symbols and landmarks of facts of belief long since lost over the generations of time.

Index